Praise for *Prayer Wasn't I*

"An honest, penetrating look at convent life in the 50's and 60's. Readers will anguish with the author in her struggle to decide whether to stay or leave the convent."

Barbara Mayer, OSB,
editor of *Benedictines* magazine.

"Dee Ready's memoir, *Prayer Wasn't Enough*, is a journey of self-discovery that allows us glimpses into the secret life of nuns, a life that is revealed to be both less dreary and more fascinating than I could have imagined!"

Melissa Ann Goodwin,
author of *The Christmas Village* and *Return to Canterbury*

"What struck me was the grace in this book. . . . Despite struggle with the silence and the discipline, she appreciates the relationships and practices she enjoyed as a nun."

Hermann Weinlick,
retired director of publications, Moravian Church in America.

". . . a 'coming-of-age story' with a unique perspective. . . . an insightful, keen awareness of the turbulent ups and downs of religious community life . . . [that] rises to a new awareness of her life, her world, and the world around her. An excellent read."

Deborah Peters, OSB,
emeritus professor of English at Benedictine College

Also by Dee Ready

A Cat's Life: Dulcy's Story

A Cat's Legacy: Dulcy's Companion Book

Prayer Wasn't Enough

A Convent Memoir

Dee Ready

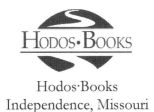

Hodos·Books
Independence, Missouri

Note to Reader: *To protect the privacy of all the nuns who were in the convent when I was there, I have used pseudonyms for them, the parishes in which I taught, and the convent.*

"O Oriens" Antiphon from *Monastic Diurnal or The Day Hours of the Monastic Breviary*, compiled by monks of St. John's Abbey, Collegeville, MN, published by H. Dessain in 1955.

Excerpt from "I thank you God for most this amazing" by e. e. cummings from *Xaipe*, published in 1950 by Oxford University Press.

Excerpt from "Prologos" by Gertrude von Le Fort from *Hymns to the Church*, published by Sheed & Ward, 1944. Translated into English by Margaret Chanler.

Excerpt from "Pied Beauty" Gerard Manley Hopkins from *Poems and Prose of Gerard Manley Hopkins*, published by Penguin Books in 1962.

"Summertime" lyric from *Porgy and Bess*, an opera composed by George Gershwin with lyrics by DuBose Heyward and Ira Gershwin, written in 1934.

Excerpt from "Abt Vogler" by Robert Browning from *Dramatic Lyrics*, published 1864.

Excerpt from "Shut Not Your Doors" by Walt Whitman from *Leaves of Grass*, final compilation of poems published in 1892.

Published by Hodos·Books
Independence, Missouri
10 9 8 7 6 5 4 1

ISBN-13: 978-1-948793-00-1

Cover photo: © Crystal Srock/Dreamstime.com
Cover design: Sally Brewer Lawrence
Book formatting for print and ebook: Linda Smitka

CONTENTS

Part III: Profession

Sister Innocence, 1963

This memoir is dedicated
to all the Benedictine nuns,
living and dead,
who welcomed me to the convent,
befriended me,
and blessed my journey when I left.
They continue   to this very day—
to pray for me.

From the depths I call to you, Yahweh:

Lord, hear my cry.

Listen attentively

To the sound of my pleading!

Psalm 130:1-2 *The New Jerusalem Bible*

Prologue

Gifted with Joy

———— ༄ ————

Never once did my parents encourage me to consider a religious vocation. Nor in sixteen years of Catholic schooling and daily Mass and Communion had I ever felt drawn to a nun's life. Their layered clothing looked hot for summer wear. Their shoes old-maidish. Convents offered no sofas or easy chairs. No going barefoot.

It seemed to me—when I thought of that life at all—to be too much togetherness; no coziness. I was used to my own creek where daily I dozed on a smooth boulder jutting from the loam-rich bank. Chilled water cascaded over my dusty feet; the sun warmed my jean-clad legs; white willows shaded my cotton T-shirt and tanned face. Time was lazy . . . and so was I.

Nuns weren't.

Yet toward the end of my junior year in college, all those negatives became as nothing to me. I had, some would say, a transcendent experience. Others might say psychotic. I know only that it set the course of my life for the next decade and beyond.

On Wednesday morning, April 10, 1957, I entered an upper-level math classroom, sat, and settled my mind on differentials. Suddenly, a silvered cloud stretched the walls of my being to the far reaches of the Universe.

Time ceased to be. No moment; no minute; no hour. I lived in the Now of Being. I felt myself weightless as the overwhelming Being of God and I became One.

Caught up as I was then in a Cloud of Oneness, Love radiated within the labyrinth of my marrow. The Cloud encapsulated me. I dwelt in a timeless, motionless Now. Yet within that Cloud dwelt the thrumming energy of all Creation. All being had become, in me, One.

Soundless words echoed within me. What I heard was not spoken. It was essence of message that entered my whole self, so that without words being spoken aloud, I knew the height, the depth, the breadth of God's gracious love.

I felt a call to pray. Ever and always. A call to let prayer become the breath within me.

A wellspring of joy swelled around and within me. No time. No space. All of me captured within the deep, dark heart of God—the Cloud that held me fast.

The next thing I knew was a tap on my shoulder, an urgent voice questioning, "Dee? Dee? Are you all right?"

Then the tap became a shaking, the voice more insistent. "Dee? Are you okay?"

I breathed. A shudder. As if from deep sleep, I stirred. I had no desire to regain momentum.

The voice persisted. My eyes focused, and I saw a friend's concerned face. Awareness pressed upon me. The hour-long math class had ended; the professor and the other students—all except Katie—were gone. I'd heard nothing; I'd been unaware of any measure called time. Presence had held me fast in soundless, radiant joy.

Looking at Katie's expression and at the mathematical formulas chalked across the blackboard, I was brought back to the classroom. Apparently everything had been routine for the other students during the last hour.

Yet everything was different for me.

As we walked down the hall, Katie said, "Dee, maybe you need to go to the infirmary. Your face's flushed."

I assured her all was well. Then, without my knowing I was going to say the words, I said, quite calmly, "I'm going to enter the convent."

"What?"

"I'm entering the convent."

"When did you decide this," Katie asked.

"Just now."

We'd come to the foyer doors. She wanted to talk more, but I said, "Katie, I need to walk outside for a while and think about this."

She nodded, grinned, then hugged me, and said, "Can I tell anyone?"

"Not yet."

"Okay." She took a few steps backward, staring at me as if she'd never before seen me. Suddenly she grinned with clear delight, then blurted, "I just can't believe it." Raising her hand in a farewell, she hurried down the hallway.

I opened the foyer's door and floated—it seemed—down the steps to the glory of flowering dogwoods beyond. Outside, my senses seemed finely tuned. The shimmer of sun on tulip yellow. The richness of pine-scented loam. The sough of wind riffling ginkgo leaves and, on my lips, the taste of gratitude. "Thank you. Thank you, God." I breathed the soundless message of Light.

A gazebo stood behind the administration building. Most students rarely visited it, but my best friend and I went there after each musical we saw at the downtown movie theater. We'd reenact every dance sequence, becoming Fred and Ginger, Gene and Debbie.

On that day—the day God called me to become a Benedictine—the gazebo beckoned. There, I skipped, spun, tapped like Gene. I was "singin' and dancin'" in a rain of joy.

It was in a cave at Subiaco, Italy, that Benedict of Nursia—born circa 480, died 543—heard his own calling. In the early sixth century, he established his first monastery. Shortly afterward, his twin sister, Scholastica, founded a convent for women.

In all the centuries between then and when I entered St. Cordelia Convent, countless men and women became Benedictines in individual communities around the world. In an ancient ceremony that took place several months after men entered a monastery or women entered a convent, they declared—professed—vows. Each did this openly before God and the other members of the community. They promised to live the vow of obedience that most monks and nuns took, as well as an implied commitment to poverty and chastity.

Benedictines also professed two additional vows. The first was to seek change within themselves for the good of all. The second was to spend their lives with the community in which they made their vows. As with all religious orders—be they those of women or men—Benedictines dedicated themselves to the work of the community they entered.

The life they lived helped Benedictines keep their vows. A large part of that life was spent in prayer. Out of this prayer flowed their commitment to the rigors of religious life—both its joys and its hardships. For centuries that passed into millennium, Benedictines met for this all-important prayer several times a day.

Through their prayer, Benedictine monks in their monasteries and Benedictine nuns in their convents offered praise and service to the God they worshiped. Throughout the Roman Catholic Church, their prayer became known as the "Divine Office" or simply, "the Office."

During the Middle Ages, that prayer led Benedictines to preserve the manuscripts that represented all the learning of the known world. Monks copied, wrote, and illuminated these manuscripts.

Not content simply to keep learning alive in their own monasteries, Benedictine monks also trekked throughout Europe as missionaries. They left the confines of the monastery in which they'd made vows so as to serve God by serving—and teaching—others.

The Rule of St. Benedict became the rule most monasteries throughout Europe used. Within those monasteries, the monks who could read became scribes. They toiled many hours a day creating libraries that housed their transcribed and embellished copies of ancient and contemporary texts.

In 1852, driven by this same desire to serve, three intrepid Benedictine nuns from Bavaria braved the tempestuous storms of the North Atlantic. With the help of Catholic families in a coastal Pennsylvania town, they built a convent. Within months, they were teaching young children from the neighboring area.

In the years that followed, spirited volunteers from that convent settled in other states. By the twentieth century Benedictine houses could be found as far west as California and as far north as the Dakotas.

In the late nineteenth century, a small group of nuns from one of those early convents traveled by train to a burgeoning town on the far western frontier. There, they established St. Cordelia Convent. In the 1920s the nuns, grown from a handful to several hundred, opened the St. Cordelia College for women.

I attended that college.

The day after I'd known the Cloud of God's Being, I knocked on the door of Sister Mary Herbert, the college dean. I didn't share with her what had happened in that math classroom the morning before. In fact, I shared that experience with no one until I began to write this memoir.

Instead, I simply asked her what I needed to do to become a Benedictine nun. She explained, then set up an appointment for me with Mother Morna Anne—the prioress, and therefore, the head of the convent.

The following Monday I walked from the college to the convent entrance, knocked, and was directed to her office; the door stood open. For a moment I just glanced around the large room, trying to encompass it. Against one side wall sat a large desk. The gooseneck lamp on its table top shone down on a stack of papers. In a straight-backed chair sat Mother Morna Anne. She smiled, beckoned me to enter, and encouraged me to sit next to her desk.

"What can I do for you, Dee?" she asked, surprising me by knowing my name.

I stammered my request, "Mother Morna Anne, I think I have a vocation . . . Well, I know I do." Her lips lifted in welcome; she nodded, encouraging me to continue.

"I want to pray. I want to be a Benedictine . . ." I stammered to an end. Once again her nod encouraged me.

"I wonder if the community," now the words came swiftly as I hurried to an end, "will accept me after I graduate from college next year."

Beaming, Mother Morna Anne rose from her chair and leaned over to embrace me. "We're happy you're answering God's call," she said.

Feeling both giddy and yet solemn, I rose and thanked her.

"We'll gladly welcome you next June," she said, taking my hand in hers. "We'll be praying for you." Then she blessed me; a deep contentment settled within my being.

Leaving her office, I walked back down a hallway in which silence reigned supreme. I would not return to that hallway until June of the following year. For a few moments I just stood there gazing at the statue of St. Benedict, which stood on a pedestal at the entrance to the convent.

The silence all around me felt like a living presence. A holy presence. Some places on Earth are steeped in holiness. They are sacred; they call us to Mystery. I felt that the motherhouse of St. Cordelia Convent was one of those places. Decades of prayer had hallowed its halls.

It was like the great European cathedrals, which a multitude of artisans had created through decades of faith-filled labor. It was like Stonehenge where ancient sages traced the passage of the sun and moon. Like Sedona, where for over eleven millennium Native Americans had lived and worked, honoring the Great Creator.

Like all these places and many more, St. Cordelia Convent blessed Earth with prayer . . . work . . . dedication.

During the following year, I continued to live in the experience I'd had in that math classroom. I felt joy. Contentment. Peace. Yet despite the persistent smile on my face, Mom stewed about my decision.

Although at that time most Catholic mothers hoped at least one daughter would enter the convent, she didn't. "You can't escape life by becoming a nun," she'd said as she mashed the supper potatoes.

"I'm not escaping."

"You're running away from your father's drinking." She added a dollop of butter.

I placed another plate on the table and said nothing. This didn't deter her.

"The thing is, Honey, people's lives get messy. That's what being human's all about. That's what's real. Life isn't all sweetness and light."

Her words hardly penetrated my ever-present jubilation.

Sighing, she said, "You retreat when things get bad." Deftly she sliced the onions for the hamburgers even as tears welled her eyes. "You go to that dream world of yours."

What she said was true. I'd always wanted to live in a home with no yelling. No knives. No ripping of Mom's dress in a drunken rage. No relatives donating canned goods, certain that Dad's shanty-Irish wife couldn't manage his hard-earned paycheck.

My mother never criticized those relatives, but I'd come to realize that Dad's mother, his two sisters, and his brother remained blind to his drinking and its consequences. They could never accept that he was an alcoholic and that when he drank whiskey he became violent.

I wanted to immerse myself in prayer and forget the terrifying scenes punctuating my childhood. Resisting reality, I held fast to the dream of a life steeped in prayer at St. Cordelia.

Glee lilted through me when I woke on Wednesday, June 25, 1958. I would be entering the convent the next day. Then I overheard Mom saying goodbye to my brother as he left for work. The night before, he and I had sat on the front stoop, saying goodbye. We'd talked about when he'd played high-school baseball and about the Blues and their standing in the Triple AAA American league. Remembering funny stories from our life together, we'd laughed as we each drank a bottle of Coke.

I'd always admired him for his ease with other people. He never met someone who didn't like him. He was the most affable person I knew, always ready to spin an Irish yarn, always ready to listen to one. Brave. Handsome. Generous.

I'd miss him greatly in the convent. Like the rest of my family, he didn't agree with the decision I'd made, but he thought the decision was mine to make.

Stuffing my arms into my robe, I raced to the front door to kiss him goodbye. While we hugged, he whispered in my ear, "Good luck."

I whispered my thank you, then said, "Will you pray for me?"

"You're the one who'll be doing the praying," he said as he let me go.

"But will you?"

"Yes."

We hugged again, holding tight. Then he kissed Mom goodbye, went out the door, got in his 1958 Chevy and drove away. It was the last time I saw him for several years. When I started crying, Mom hugged me. We swayed back and forth together until she said, "You go get dressed; I'll get breakfast on the table."

While Mom cooked the last meal I'd eat at home, I dressed in the uniform I'd wear for the next six months—my months as a postulant in the convent. During that time, I'd be on probation. The convent and I would determine if the life of a nun was suitable for me.

First, I donned black lisle hose. Then came my everyday cotton panties, bra, and slip. Next I slipped on and buttoned a long-sleeved black blouse and stepped into a pleated black skirt that covered my knobby knees. Over the blouse went a white-collared black cape that fell to my wrists. On my size 7 ½ feet I wore black oxfords. A comb sewn to a black veil anchored my flyaway hair.

Feeling newly arrived in the world, I walked into the kitchen where Mom was dishing up my breakfast. I twirled like Debbie and Ginger so that the hem of my skirt flared out into the space between the door and table. Stretching to my full five-foot-and-four-inch height, I asked, "How do you think I look? Do I look like someone who wants to be a nun?"

"I like you better in lavender," she said. "It's your favorite color."

"I know, but do I look okay in black?"

"You look fine. They're lucky to have you." With that, she set on the table a bowl of oatmeal with raisins and crunchy black walnuts from our backyard tree.

I fetched milk from the refrigerator, sat down at the dining-room table, and picked up the morning newspaper. Aware I'd never get to read one again, I absorbed the articles and features. The front page announced the latest disagreement between the Democratic congress and Dwight D. Eisenhower, the Republican president. In France, Charles de Gaulle had come out of retirement to deal with the Algerian problem.

I argued with the editorial that day, then read aloud to Mom two letters from readers. Next I turned to my favorite comics: "Blondie," "Dick Tracy," "Brenda Starr," "Popeye," "Peanuts," "The Adventures of Smilin' Jack," "Pogo."

Seeing the time, I relinquished the routine I'd practiced since I was eight. It was then Dad had introduced me to the daily satisfaction of reading a newspaper. I folded the last copy I thought I'd ever hold and placed it on the seat of his easy chair.

While I'd read, Mom had been checking my suitcase to be sure I had all the clothes listed on the information sheet the convent had provided. On each article of clothing she'd sewn my nametag— DR3. The initials and number indicated I would be the third living person in the convent whose name before entering began with those letters.

Besides clothing, the suitcase also held the three books I'd use for prayer in the convent: my daily missal for Mass and two books for praying with the other nuns. Three friends had given me these books as a graduation gift. They'd written their names inside so I'd remember to pray for them; I'd promised never to forget.

Dad woke later than usual. It was a day he'd dreaded, and he hadn't gotten up to eat breakfast or say goodbye to my brother. While I'd read the newspaper, Mom had gone into their bedroom to tell him it was time to dress. I was nearly ready to leave when Mr. Simonet arrived to pick him up. The two of them worked construction on a downtown skyscraper. Hearing the car's horn, Dad came out of the bedroom.

When I turned from the suitcase to say my goodbyes, he put his long arms around me, holding me close. He stood nearly a foot taller than I, so as my face rested against his chest, I could hear his heart beating.

My father had always loved me. He'd never laid a hand on me except once he'd slapped me when I sassed my mother. Always he'd bragged about me in the smoke-filled bars where he sat boozing in a booth until the bartender announced, "Last glass, Folks." Only then would Dad drive home, weaving back and forth across the road.

Many times as a young child I'd been in the backseat of the Chevy coupe with my brother, while Mom sat rigid in the front. His driving had frightened me. When we'd get home, he'd stagger across the room, sometimes collapsing on the couch, other times making it to the bedroom and tumbling onto the bed. Or he'd start an argument with Mom that could become violent at any time. My brother and I cowered on the couch, afraid to move.

The next day he'd come to the table ashamed, gazing down at his plate, saying nothing, nor did we. The night before, which had been typical, was over. We'd try for a new day. During all the years of my childhood, Dad hoped that my life would be much easier than his had been. Now I was leaving to become a nun—a bitter disappointment. I would never marry or have a family of my own.

"You'll be locked away," he'd grumbled when I told him and Mom I was entering. "It's like they say, 'When the monks rape the nuns, babies get adopted.'" I gasped at such a skewed view of the convent, but that's what Dad believed. "You'll be one of those robots," he insisted, "A raped robot."

For several weeks he watched as Mom and I prepared my clothes and read the convent's prep sheet, but he said nothing. Mostly he simply sat in his armchair, staring out the window.

In the past month, I'd had to tell Dad he'd be allowed to visit me only once each year. He knew I'd return home for a visit only if he, Mom, or my brother were gravely ill. For the past weeks, the strictness of this rule had left him mute about my leaving. Now the waiting was over.

Mr. Simonet honked again; they were running late. Holding tight, Dad whispered, "This will always . . . it will always . . . I mean always . . . be your home."

He let his arms fall, wiped away tears, and walked out to where Mr. Simonet waited in his black Buick. While Dad stared dismally at me through the windshield, Mr. Simonet backed his car down the rutted driveway out onto Geyser Road. I stood in the doorway, waving goodbye.

As soon as they left, Mom and I got into our rust-pocked '48 Chevy and drove away from the farm where I'd spent much of my childhood. In early September and late May for the last four years, Mom had driven me to and from St. Cordelia College, so she knew how long the trip would take.

Neither Mom nor I spoke much during our journey. I don't know what she was thinking because I didn't ask. I was too caught up in my own thoughts: *What would happen when we got to the convent? How many other young women would be entering? Would the nuns accept me when the time came to vote on my staying?*

The most important question to me at the time was "Will I have to keep quiet all the time?" Like my brother, I loved to weave stories. I wasn't sure how well I'd succeed with silence, but if that was what a nun had to do, I'd do it. Willingly. I'd do anything so that I could live a life of prayer.

Later that afternoon we stopped at a motel to spend the night. The next morning, we arrived at the convent's motherhouse a little after 11:00 a.m. I took my suitcase from the back seat and turned toward my new home. Accompanying me to its wide front porch,

Mom knocked at the massive door. Within moments, a welcoming nun opened it, introducing herself as Sister Elena.

"I'll be your novice mistress," she said. "You and the other postulants as well as the novices will be living in the novitiate next door. We'll go there after Vespers."

I had no idea what she meant. No idea what a postulant or a novice was. No idea that I'd live in a building called the novitiate. No idea what a *novice mistress* did. I did know that Vespers was the prayer the nuns chanted after the noon meal.

After inviting us into the foyer, Sister Elena carried my suitcase into the main hall. In her brief absence, Mom turned to me.

"Dolores," she said, "you're my daughter, and I'm happy for you because you're happy. Please, just remember how much your dad and I love you. Don't forget," she added, "that you can always come home. Anytime. Just call."

Throughout my life, she'd been my anchor. Now I was leaving her behind. We'd be permitted to exchange letters only once a month. I dreaded our separation, but prayer beckoned.

When Sister Elena returned, she shook Mom's hand, thanking her for giving a daughter to the convent. After we embraced one last time, Mom left. Through the door window, I watched as she walked slowly toward the car. For a moment, a longing for one last look at her face—the beauty of it, the serenity—overwhelmed me. I took a deep breath, remembered my reason for being there, turned, and entered the convent.

The next chapter of my life began.

Part I

The Novitiate

A Welcomed Routine

Sister Elena led me down the first-floor hallway to a parlor where several other young women sat, each dressed alike. Sister Elena said, "Sit here with the other postulants, Dee. This is a time of silence so please do not talk among yourselves." I nodded my understanding.

Turning to the rest of the young women, she said, "Mother will give salutation during the mid-day meal. You'll get to talk and visit then." Another new word was added to my growing list: *salutation*. I knew that those of us entering were postulants, but I still didn't know what a novice was.

Before leaving, Sister Elena explained a little more: "At your dining-room table will be sixteen novices. They have been here for a year and now wear the habit."

She gazed at us for a moment and added, "Their white veils are the sign that they are novices. You'll get to talk with them at lunch also." She then turned back into the hall. In the next half hour or so, she led three more postulants into the room where we all sat in silence.

By the time the bell rang for lunch, eighteen of us had gathered in that room. Later I learned that the other seventeen postulants had come, as I had, because they felt called to serve God as a Benedictine. To serve God and to seek to find Him within themselves and others. Several of them were recent high school graduates. Others, like myself, had been in college. Still others, working a variety of jobs, had heard the call to religious life and responded.

Feeling both nervous and excited, I walked with them as we followed Sister Elena down a side hall and into the silence of the summer dining room. There I witnessed a sea of beaming faces. I wanted to shout, "I'm here! I'm home!"

I felt beautiful that day. I felt that Dee Ready, in her black skirt and cape, had disappeared and all that was left was Joy. I was setting out on a lifelong voyage of discovery. For all the years that lay ahead, I would praise the great, good God of all creation in and through the vows I'd soon profess. He had sought me out; now I sought to know Him more deeply and to let him probe the very depths of my being.

I'd always felt that God accompanied me wherever I was. He was there when I laughed with others, did my homework, prepared for bed. He was always on the right side of my body, near enough for me to reach down and touch his fur.

This awareness had been with me since I was five and first met Arthur, my imaginary lion friend. That year—from September 1941 to August 1942—had been a terrifying one for me. I'd felt that my parents, in moving to another city with my brother and leaving me behind, had abandoned me. My grandmother told me so.

Then one day, as I walked to school through a field of tall weeds, Arthur padded toward me. I learned early on that no one else saw this magnificent lion against whose stomach I lay my head at night. As I drifted into sleep, I could feel his gentle heart beat beneath my cheek.

No one saw him lying on the floor next to my kindergarten desk. No one saw him walk me home. None of that mattered: I saw him. I knew the comfort he brought me. I heard his voice assuring me that all was well. That I was safe.

In August my parents returned, but Arthur stayed with me. He was present when I had asthma attacks and got behind in school. He lay on the boulders by the creek as I rested against him and read.

As the years passed I saw Arthur less and less until I could see him no longer, but I knew his presence accompanied me to the final years of grade school and into high school and college. He had become the God who walked beside me. His presence was always there. I felt that I walked in a cloud of protective Presence.

When the experience in the math classroom happened, I knew what Arthur—the God who loved me to giddiness—desired of me. A little over a year later—on Thursday, June 26, 1958—I jubilantly walked into the summer dining room. Within it, stood four long, rectangular tables covered with white tablecloths. Nuns with black veils sat at three of those tables. Given Sister Elena's earlier speech, I recognized that the women in white veils, who sat at the table on the far right, were novices.

Light streamed into the room from three walls of windows. Everyone was smiling at us, but no one spoke. Silence reigned. We postulants shattered that silence as we pulled back our chairs at the novices' table and took our places. The chairs screeched against the wooden floor; I felt myself cringing at the sound. After we'd settled ourselves, we sat in silence as several nuns presented us with large bowls and platters of food.

Then, over the loudspeaker, someone said, "Praise be Jesus and Mary."

Everyone responded with "Now and forever. Amen."

Loud chattering followed these words. We postulants glanced at one another, unsure why conversations were blossoming throughout the room. Chuckling, a nearby novice encouraged us to speak. "Mother just gave us salutation." she confided. "So it's okay to talk."

None of us had any idea what *salutation* really meant but we all began to jabber. Only later did we learn that when the prioress "saluted" us with "Praise be Jesus and Mary," she was giving us permission to talk.

Immediately after dinner, over six hundred nuns, clad in floor-length, black serge habits and white coif and forehead bands, walked silently, in two rows, down the hall and entered the chapel to pray. Sister Elena, the white-veiled novices—they, too, in the floor-length black habit—and we short-skirted postulants followed behind. Once there, each postulant sat next to a novice.

I was next to Sister Agatha. She demonstrated how to reverently kiss my diurnal—the book I'd be using whenever the community met for prayer—and how to turn the tissue-thin pages without leaving oily smudges. With her prompting, I began to chant. I felt piercing delight; prayer satisfied my soul as nothing else had ever done.

After praying the four psalms that comprised Vespers that day, we eighteen postulants and the sixteen novices walked silently down the main hallway of the convent. We descended the steps to the basement, opened the outside door, and then ascended steps to the ground level. Silently we walked across the driveway that separated the main convent from a much smaller two-story, brick building. It was, I soon learned, the novitiate where I would spend the next eighteen months.

In the days that followed I also learned that the convent's four-story building, where we'd eaten lunch, had been built at the turn of the century. The first floor of what was called "the motherhouse" contained office space, the refectories or dining rooms, an expansive kitchen, and the sculleries where the nuns washed dishes. Dorms, private rooms, bathrooms, lavatories, utility rooms, an infirmary, and the library occupied the three other floors. The choir chapel stood at the north end of the main building.

At the south end, on a slight rise and across the driveway from the motherhouse, stood the novitiate. It was the residence of the postulants (those of us who'd just entered), the novices (those who had been there for a year and were preparing to make first vows in six months), the novice mistress (who would teach us the Rule of St. Benedict and the traditions of St. Cordelia's), and the assistant novice mistress who helped her.

The driveway that separated the novitiate from the motherhouse led to the cemetery. Beyond it, gardens and orchards produced fruit and vegetables for the nuns' daily meals.

The man who'd owned this property, before the nuns arrived in this frontier town, had built, behind his Victorian home, a carriage house. It now served as the convent's laundry. For the next eighteen months, I'd spend two days a week there. The college now used the Victorian home as its music department.

On that first day, after we'd chanted our prayers and been led to the novitiate, Sister Elena gathered us in the first-floor recreation room. There she gave us an overview of the linchpin of the Order of St. Benedict—the Divine Office.

As we sat in two rows, she stood before us, clasping a diurnal. "The early sixth-century Benedictines met at various times—or hours—of the day for prayer," she began. "We follow that tradition. We use this book, a diurnal, to pray those hours."

I felt gleeful as I looked at the book she held. I'd be using a diurnal—one of the books given to me by my college friends— each day, every day, for the rest of my life.

"Throughout each day, we chant Lauds, Prime, Terce, Sext, None, Vespers, Matins, and Compline. We call this the Liturgy of the Hours," she explained.

Raising my hand, I asked, "Sister Elena, will we spend our whole day in chapel? Or most of it? That is, eight hours of it?"

"No, Dee," she said, smiling broadly. "The word *hours* as used here simply mean times. We meet several times a day to pray. During one of those times, we pray three 'hours' sequentially. That takes only about fifteen minutes. Sometimes, as with Matins, we do pray nearly an hour."

Next, she explained just when we'd meet for prayer. "The first hour for us here at St. Cordelia's Convent is Lauds. That word means 'to praise.' I want you to always remember that we start our day with psalms of praise. We start with Lauds; afterward, we celebrate Mass, which is a prayer of thanksgiving."

She turned and printed the word *Lauds* on the chalkboard behind her.

"Questions?" she asked.

When none of us raised our hand, she continued, "After Mass each day, we pray the hour of Prime, which lasts about ten minutes. Then we leave the chapel . . . in silence . . . and walk down the hall to the dining room where we eat breakfast."

She chalked the word *Prime* on the board.

One or two postulants began to whisper, and I heard "Food" and "Finally, we get to eat!"

Sister Elena's voice silenced us. "Remember, unless you are given salutation—and I haven't done that—you stay silent." Those words effectively cut off any whispering we felt like doing.

"After breakfast," she continued, "we do our obediences, which I'll explain later. Then we meet again in chapel and pray Terce, Sext, and None." She paused to chalk these three words on the board.

Turning back toward us, she said, "These are the three hours that together take only about fifteen minutes. Then . . . ," she actually grinned at us as she said, "you'll get to eat again. Dinner!" I found myself liking her immensely.

"After dinner," she explained, "we file in silence down the hall to the choir chapel where we will . . . ."

When she said that, one of the other postulants quickly raised her hand and asked, "Do we get to talk at dinner?" Sister Elena nodded.

Another postulant quickly asked, "Is that the first time we get to talk all morning?" Again Sister Elena, with a glint of amusement in her eyes, nodded.

So no talking for hours. We would voice out loud only our prayers.

Once again she printed a word on the chalkboard: *Vespers.* "This word means 'evening song.' Benedictines used to gather in chapel at dusk to chant the Vesper psalms. However, when we started teaching, we needed to change our schedule. Now we pray Vespers after lunch. It's another hour in which we use psalms to praise God for all that has been and is."

Once again, she paused. Looking around, she asked, "Which hours are left?"

"Matins and Compline," the postulant at the left end of the first row said.

"Correct. The monks in their monasteries and the Benedictine nuns in their convents used to rise before the sun to pray the psalms and do the readings for Matins. It's a word that means 'belonging to the morning.' The hour of Matins was meant to end at dawn. Do you have any idea why we pray it in the late afternoon?"

I ventured a guess. "Because Benedictines need a full night's sleep if they're going to teach the next day?"

"Yes. A full night's sleep is necessary. We now gather to pray Matins in the afternoon. Then we have supper. After that we come back here to the novitiate and recreate. We talk. Play board games. Darn our socks. Relax."

As I contemplated the day, I realized that the evening recreation was really the first time we could relax. I was going to be busy praying and eating and also doing something called "obediences"— whatever they were.

"What's the final hour of the day?" Sister Elena asked.

"Compline!" several of us said, with just a tinge of a shout in our voice.

"Right! It's my favorite hour of the day. The word means 'to complete.' When the community meets for Compline we offer praise and thanksgiving for the day's gifts." She looked at each one of us individually and then added, "Remember that. We are grateful for the day—no matter what has happened—and we thank God for it."

Like myself, the other postulants seemed eager to grab hold of just what our life was going to be for the next eighteen months. Our hands rose almost as one to ask questions. Immediately, Sister Elena requested our patience. She wanted us first to follow her upstairs to the two dorms—one for novices, the other for postulants. We were to walk in silence until she gave us salutation at an appropriate time.

Sister Elena led us into the postulants' dorm, stepped aside, and let us view it in silence. She whispered that the convent allowed no talking in the dorm. We would leave this dorm in the morning and not return until bedtime.

As I looked around, I saw a series of horizontal pipes fitted into four vertical poles. These sectioned our dorm into twenty cells. White canvas-like curtains hung from the horizontal poles. A series of windows along the west and south walls faced each cell.

Sister Elena demonstrated how we were to pull these curtains closed to create our individual cells. Each of these housed a straight-backed chair, a twin bed, and a two-drawer dresser on which sat a wide ceramic bowl. In a whisper, she said, "You are to close these curtains whenever you dress or undress. Draw the curtains open when you leave the dorm for the day and right before you settle into bed at night."

Finally, Sister Elena assigned our cells. I would sleep in the sixth one from the door. As she assigned cells to the remaining postulants, I stood by my bed and looked out the open window. Beyond, children played in a neighboring yard. Their laughter cascaded into the dorm.

The remainder of the day consisted of more instruction, the hour-long prayer of Matins in the college chapel, an evening meal, recreation, and Compline—the final prayer of the day. After that evening prayer, the novices and the postulants, I among them, silently returned to the novitiate.

That first night in the convent set the pattern for every other night that followed: In profound silence, we climbed the steps to the second-story dorms. In that "Grand Silence," each of us filled a basin with water and set the ceramic bowl on our bureau.

Next, we pulled closed the white curtains to create our own living space. We removed our clothing, arranged it on the back of the straight-backed chair, dressed in our nightgowns, pulled open the curtains, and climbed into bed. Sister Elena turned off the light. As I fell into sleep, the sun was setting beyond the open window by my bed.

The next morning, while stars still pinned the dark heavens to the Universe, a bell summoned us to wake. We drew the curtains around our beds, washed in our basin of water, donned our clothes, drew the curtains aside, emptied the water in the lavatory sinks, made our beds, and silently gathered with the novices in the first-floor hallway.

Together, we marched in two rows across the driveway to the convent basement entrance. Mounting the steps to the first floor hall, we walked down it to the college chapel. There we chanted Lauds, celebrated Mass, prayed Prime, left the chapel, and ate breakfast in the dining room.

During the remainder of the day a bell announced meals, classes, prayer, and recreation. In the evening it rang for Compline—the final "hour" of the day. This routine became my daily life—one of obedience steeped in prayer, work, and silence. A ringing bell bookended each day's beginning and ending.

On Sunday, our routine varied a little. We still met several times a day to pray the Divine Office and to eat, but we dressed in Sunday clothes and relaxed in the novitiate or the side yard. Often, a novice or a postulant left the group because her family had come to visit.

The first Sunday of every month, however, was a day of silence and retreat. We met individually with the novice mistress to discuss any concerns we might have or any suggestions she might have for our living the religious life more fully.

During the evening of those first Sundays, Sister Elena handed out any mail we'd received in the preceding month. Afterward, we shared a delicious treat provided by the parents of a nun who'd been in the novitiate several years before. Her family had a standing order with a local bakery for two or three lavishly decorated layered cakes for each first Sunday. We all looked forward to those sumptuous cakes.

A few days after we entered, a postulant from Colorado impulsively blurted, "We keep getting dessert. Every night! At home we only get dessert on Christmas and Easter." Because we never talked about our families, I had no idea that some of us hadn't eaten as well as others. Her sharing was a revelation to me.

This not talking about the past was a convent tradition I found particularly difficult. We'd left the secular world behind. All that went on there—even with our families—was meant to stay there and be no part of our conversations during recreation.

The convent discouraged us from talking about our school days or the friends we'd left behind. Nor did we share any of the experiences that might have led us to the convent. We didn't discuss any jobs we'd had or vacations or family stories or hopes and dreams.

We never wondered together about what was happening in the world beyond the motherhouse. Were there wars? Revolutions? Recessions? Elections? We didn't know.

We discussed only our daily classes and any mishaps we'd had doing the tasks Sister Elena had assigned us. This brought forth laughter; in fact, we laughed a lot. We were spirited young women engaged in a great venture—seeking God. The convent's rules kept us living in the here and now of religious life. By doing that we lived in Presence—the presence of the God we were seeking.

Both in high school and college, I'd enjoyed learning about friends' lives, about what had made them who they were. Given this mandate not to share the past, however, I learned little about the background of the other postulants or novices. At times, however, I'd learn some small tidbit that helped me better understand a classmate.

This happened when the eighteen-year-old Colorado postulant inadvertently spoke of desserts in her home. Also, when families visited, I might see brothers and sisters gathered around a postulant or novice.

Our families could visit us only once during the summer. They came to the main convent building and someone fetched us from the novitiate. We then spent two or three hours visiting while sitting on benches amidst the pine trees. None of us—postulants, novices, scholastics, or professed—ate with our families, but we welcomed just seeing them and catching up on the news.

When Mom and Dad came to visit me in August, I interrogated them about what was happening in the world beyond the confines of the convent. They'd be voting in the November election. Who was running for Congress? What did his chances look like? What about my cousins? What were they doing? And how was Kentucky, my brother's dog? Questions poured out of me.

That visit had to satisfy me until I'd see my parents again in late December for the ceremony in which I'd receive the habit. For the remainder of 1958, I wouldn't see them again or learn any news.

Each Sunday but the first one of the month, one other postulant, two novices, and I became downright cunning. When families visited the professed nuns as well as the scholastics, they would often meander to the cemetery to view the large sculpture there and to pass beneath the arching branches of the oak trees lining the driveway. As they walked, many of these visitors smoked.

Sisters Michael and Deanna, both novices, and Ruth, a postulant, had smoked before entering. They sorely missed their "ciggies." So after supper on each of those visiting Sundays, four of us from the novitiate would amble down that driveway. Our mission? Salvaging the butts.

Afterward, we'd huddle behind the trees. I—the nonsmoking asthmatic—stood alert. The other three, facing away from the convent buildings, pulled their veils around their faces, and lit up. After their first inhalation, I'd hear the satisfied, "Ah!"

Each Sunday during those summer months we rescued thirty or so butts. Afterward, my three friends divided the butts equally. The following Sunday, we'd fill our pockets again. The three of them hoarded what they could of their bounty for the days that followed.

The Benedictine convent I entered celebrated its centennial in 1963. I have no idea if, during those one hundred years, other nuns reclaimed cigarette butts and smoked them. Whether they did or not, meant little to me. Those three fellow sojourners blowing smoke rings gave me memories that lightened my spirits in the novitiate.

Living in that convent with them and all the other nuns, I knew moments of rich laughter and profound joy. I also knew moments of doubt, but that came later in my eighteen-month sojourn, first as a postulant and then as a novice.

One of the first things Sister Elena explained to us after we entered the convent was the "making of culpa." That is, the admitting of a fault or flaw. For instance, if we spoke during periods of silence—especially during the grand silence between the last prayer of the day and the first of the morning—that was disregard for the Rule. Other infractions would be losing a straight pin—that was a failure to live poverty—or talking while doing dishes—that was breaking silence.

Culpa matters encompassed both the large and small: dropping a book and disturbing the peace of others, slamming a door, staining our clothes or the dining-room tablecloth. All had to do with taking poverty seriously and respecting everyone's need for silence so as to focus on God's presence.

When we'd neglected to observe a rule or tradition, we knocked on Sister Elena's door, entered, knelt beside where she sat, and said, "Mea culpa, I spoke during the grand silence. If Jesus wills it, may I have a penance?" With those first two words, we were admitting we'd made a mistake and it was our fault.

Sister Elena would then say something like, "Go to the chapel this evening during recreation and pray." Or, "Sweep the stairs and pick up all the pins you find. Bring them to me." Or, "Say an 'Our Father' for the community."

In Sister Elena's office, I daily admitted my failures with regard to following and living the Rule of St. Benedict. Both day and night, I practiced custody of the eyes by not staring at whatever or whomever I passed. The hope was that by doing so, I'd center my mind on spiritual things and thus live in the present. If I did so, I would be mindful of the Rule and what I was doing throughout the day.

With input from Sister Elena and her hawk's eye, we picked a virtue or action to work on each month so as to be more observant in living the Rule. We kept a journal in which to record our daily problems with the particular virtue we'd chosen. At the end of each month we presented this journal to Sister Elena and together decided what we needed to work on for the coming month.

Very early on she and I decided that I needed to work on discretion. The conversation went something like this:

"Dee, during recreation last night, you talked right over what Jessie was saying."

"I'm sorry. . . . I wasn't aware."

"That's just it. You weren't aware. Often you just open your mouth and say whatever you're thinking. More often what you say is extremely inappropriate."

I knew this was true. I was impulsive. When I had a thought, it would come tumbling out of my mouth.

"What bothers me most," she said, "is that you sometimes say things that show you aren't centered in the moment. You need to learn to think before speaking. You really need to practice an inner silence that isn't yet a part of you."

I could say nothing to this; it was all true. "You want me to be less spontaneous?" I asked.

"I'd like you to work on being discreet."

I spent the majority of the next sixteen months working on discretion. During that time, I never once made culpa for snagging cigarette butts—that involved other people.

On the other hand, nearly every day, I was in Sister Elena's office, kneeling and saying the same thing, "Mea culpa, I was indiscreet again. I . . ." Then would follow the doleful tale of my misdemeanor.

The Heartwish of Prayer

The motto of the Benedictine Order is "Ora et labora," that is, pray and work. For Benedictines, prayer is the main work of the monastery. It is their daily praise of the God whom they serve. They serve this God by serving others and by the willingness and obedience they bring to their work throughout each and every day. Thus, manual and intellectual labor becomes prayer. For a Benedictine, prayer is work offered to God; work is prayer offered with the same spirit of reverence.

During the summer months in the convent, all the nuns were home from their mission schools. Because of the increased number, we prayed in the college chapel. It was a large Romanesque church of great beauty with soaring heights and intricately carved columns. Its stained glass windows cast jeweled lozenges of color on the gleaming polished floor and the satiny wood of the pews. These faced the altar above which hung the gray sculptured marble form of a crucified, but profoundly serene, Jesus of Nazareth.

The majority of the nuns departed each fall for their teaching missions. After they left for nine months, the remaining nuns met for prayer in the smaller choir chapel that stood at one end of the motherhouse. Spaced on its long side walls, luminescent stained-glass windows welcomed light. The hue of each pane touched lightly the palette of color. Each window illustrated one aspect of the life and the Rule of our founder: St. Benedict of Nursia.

Beneath these windows stood four stepped tiers of stalls. The top stalls rested against the two long side walls. Running down the chapel's length and separating the tiers on each side was a wide, linoleum-surfaced aisle. The stalls on the left of this aisle faced the ones on the right.

The straight-backed stalls had a narrow, separating partition on each side. The wooden seat of each stall was hinged so we could swing it upright to provide more room for standing as we prayed. In front of each seat a small, freestanding kneeler sat on the floor. A cubbyhole was built into the back of the seats in the tier below.

In the cubbyhole of my assigned stall, I kept my missal, used during daily Mass, and also my diurnal, from which I chanted the 150 psalms of the Hebrew Bible each week. Numerous prayers, readings, and hymns supplemented those psalms. While praying the Divine Office, we chanted these psalm verses antiphonally—first one side, then the other.

We stood as one, bowed as one, knelt as one, or sat as one during different parts of the Office, which we chanted in Latin. When all of us were in good voice, the chanted prayer lifted our hearts beyond things like public culpa, giggling, and noisy kneelers. Our bodies cast weariness aside. Peace anointed us. That is the truest thing I can say—that the choir chapel was a place of peace. For nearly a century before I entered, women had prayed there. Their praise had become Presence.

At the day's ending, nuns who'd diminished that peace and the praise offered to God that day made public culpa during Compline. We would kneel in the aisle, bow our heads, and silently ask forgiveness from the community. Several disturbances might result in a nun—or nuns—kneeling in that aisle.

Giggling. Next to me in chapel sat a fellow postulant with whom I shared the same sense of humor. Little things set us off, like the way a nun sneezed or even the way she blew her nose.

Banging the kneeler during Mass or while chanting disturbed the other nuns in their prayer and was a culpa matter.

Mangling a Latin word undermined the beauty of our prayer and the peace that permeated it.

Chanting off-key. What I quickly discovered is that my ear simply didn't recognize pitch.

At least once a week, I left my stall and knelt in the aisle during Compline. Sometimes, I had giggled during prayer; often I mangled the Latin or chanted off-key, but the most frequent cause behind my sojourn in the aisle was the banging of the kneeler. I simply had always been awkward. As I stumbled and bumbled through my childhood, Mom uttered in frustration, "Dolores, you've got two left feet!" That clumsiness didn't magically change in the convent. I continued to drop dishes, walk into walls, stumble over kneelers.

Throughout the eighteen months of the novitiate I consciously tried to counter this tendency by being aware every moment that Arthur padded with me down the hall and into chapel, dining room, kitchen, scullery, classroom, or laundry. Only through this awareness did my awkwardness enter abeyance. Often as I walked down a hallway, my eyes downcast, I would feel as if Arthur and I danced together down the yellow brick road. At the end of that corridor awaited, not the Emerald City, but a place of profound peace—the choir chapel.

There is no denying that during the year and a half of the novitiate, a thin thread of indecision wove its way through the tapestry of my intent. Despite that, each evening at Compline I let go of doubt and settled into the peace that spanned the fifteen centuries from Benedict at Subiaco, just forty miles from Rome and the Tiber, to Dee Ready at St. Cordelia's, just a hop, skip, and jump from another river—one in the New World. That centuries-old peace permeated the very words I chanted to end the day.

Whenever I was in the choir chapel, I could feel the Oneness of all those who had gone before me, all those who would come after, and all those with whom I then lived. In that chapel, I became One with All Creation. That is to say, I experienced the soundless message of God's deep, dark love given to me in the math classroom the year before.

Most of the women in the convent I entered taught in schools scattered around several neighboring states. Each August they traveled by car or train to the mission where they'd spend the upcoming nine months. Their assigned work, or obedience, was to teach in the grade and/or high school of the Catholic parish in which the mission convent was located.

The postulants and novices, I among them, stayed home in the convent. Mother Morna Anne entrusted Sister Elena, our novice mistress, with assigning obediences for us: cleaning, table-waiting, dishwashing, and working in the laundry among them.

The one I most enjoyed was keeping shipshape a two-stall lavatory in the main convent building of the motherhouse. When Sister Elena assigned this task to Carrie and me, we two postulants quickly recognized its fringe benefits: damp newspapers—those very newspapers I thought I'd never hold in my hands again.

Scholastics and professed nuns had used these newspapers for getting rid of spots on their scapulars. This was an article of clothing they wore over their habit—an ankle-length, black serge, long-sleeved dress. A scapular consisted of two identical pieces of black serge. On average, each piece was five feet long and twenty inches wide with a hemmed arc at one end for encircling the neck. The two pieces were sewn together at the neck on one side of the shoulders; they snapped on the other side so a nun could easily don the scapular. It covered both the front and the back of the habit and kept it from being soiled.

When a nun stained a scapular by perhaps dropping a morsel of greasy food on it, she'd come to the restroom. There she'd wash the scapular in the sink, wring it out, then roll it in layers of newspaper to absorb any excess water. Later she'd iron the garment and leave behind the damp papers, stained black from the scapular's dye.

This was the treasure trove Carrie and I found each day in the restroom's wastepaper basket. On that first day of discovery, we stood amazed. For us, this was clearly not an obedience, but an opportunity.

The convent strictly forbade reading newspapers, watching television, or listening to the radio. Postulants concentrated instead on learning how to leave the secular world behind. Carrie and I had willingly done so but sorely missed the news. Both of us hungered to know what was happening in the wide world beyond the convent walls.

Those newspapers tempted us. Reading them would be against the rules; not reading them seemed impossible. If caught, we'd get in trouble, maybe Sister Elena would even ask us to leave the convent. We didn't know for sure. What we did know is that news of the outside world awaited us if we but dared. We had to devise a plan. We knew that concealment was essential to our continued presence in the convent. Or so we believed.

That night during recreation, she and I plotted how we'd manage our escapade. We needed a way to each take a turn cleaning and a turn reading and to do so without being caught. The next day we put into plan into action.

Once we'd entered the lavatory to begin our obedience, Carrie began to clean the toilet in the second stall, the two sinks, and the windows. While she did that I took my turn reading. First, I retrieved from the wastebasket a damp newspaper. Then I entered the first stall. Latching the door behind me, I stepped up on the toilet seat and steadied myself, one foot on each side of the rim. Straddling carefully, I squatted low so my head was well below the top of the stall door. Quickly, I scanned the news, deciphering words through the black blotches.

When a professed nun came into the lavatory and tried to open the door of the stall in which I was squatting, I heard Carrie break silence by whispering, "Sister, that stall has a faulty toilet in it. Because of that, I've locked the door." The nun must have nodded her understanding, because she entered the stall next to mine without saying anything to Carrie. I held my breath as I heard the nun latch the door, do her business, then close the door behind her, wash her hands, and depart.

We'd done it! Perhaps the door of the first stall being locked from the inside had puzzled that nun, but seemingly, she never suspected Carrie of being devious. A postulant wouldn't fib. Surely not. Ha!

After she left, Carrie and I, grinning at one another, proud of our ingenuity, traded places. I cleaned and emptied the wastepaper basket into the hall bins, dusted the shades, and mopped the bathroom floor.

When I finished these tasks, I tapped on the door. "Carrie," I whispered, "it's all clean except for that toilet." She opened the stall door and emerged with a smile on her face. Deftly she cleaned the toilet bowl. Then we left the restroom and returned to the novitiate.

We'd done it! We'd read the newspapers and not gotten caught. Clearly, we had a quintessential plan: Stand. Stoop. Straddle. Squat. Read. As the months of our postulancy passed, she and I perfected this maneuver with nary a word from anyone. Both of us got to read each day. Moreover, with a mop as my partner, I got to dance as I swabbed the terrazzo floors.

From Compline the night before to lunch the next day, we did not speak unless it was absolutely necessary. We ate breakfast in silence. In fact, we were silent until lunch. For that meal and supper, we began silently while the nun at the head of each table passed around a plate of homemade bread. Each of us took at least half a slice. We then cut off the top crust and divided it into five or three pieces.

The five pieces were in remembrance of the wounds of a crucified Jesus: his nailed hands, his feet, and his pierced side. The three pieces honored the Trinity: Father, Son, and Holy Spirit. We placed the remainder of the half slice on the tablecloth next to our plate and used it as a resting place for our silverware. Doing so kept the cloth clean.

Meanwhile, the six servers, each with a large tray on wheels, entered the dining room. As quietly as possible, they wheeled the trays to the tables they were serving and passed out bowls of vegetables, platters of meat, and a gravy bowl. While these nuns— novices during the school year and scholastics in the summer— served the dinner and supper meals, the nun who'd been appointed the reader for that week read aloud, using a microphone, from whatever spiritual book the prioress had chosen.

During my first autumn in the novitiate, one of the books was a history of missionary work in Africa. For the first time I heard the word *Hottentots*, the seventeenth-century name white Europeans gave to the Khoikhoi people of Africa. The book never mentioned that the term was pejorative.

With so many hours of silence, we postulants latched onto anything that seemed funny. The repetition of the letter "t" and the cadence of the word *Hottentot* seemed hilariously funny to us. For days that passed into weeks, whenever anyone in the laundry glanced up from her work and saw another postulant looking her way, she'd mouth "Hottentot!" They'd both giggle delightedly, unaware of being offensive.

After the reading for lunch and supper, the prioress gave us salutation. With permission to talk, we turned to one another, our words tumbling out, all of us eager to share whatever happened when we'd done our obediences. Of course, Carrie and I never mentioned those damp newspapers and our ingenious plan.

A superior did not give salutation for breakfast or during certain seasons of the Church year for the two other meals. Except for those seasons, however, we talked during dinner and supper. We also spoke aloud to one another for a short while after Vespers and in the evening during recreation. Other than that, we observed silence.

We ended each meal by wiping the remnants of food and juices from our plates with the remainder of the half slice we'd used. Then we ate this soaked morsel along with the three or five pieces on our plate. This practice helped with the dishwashing.

Afterward, the table servers brought around towels, wide-handled metal tin cups containing hot soapy water, and a diminutive washing mop. They placed the cup on each side of the table. The two novices at the front end of the table—to the right and left of Sister Elena—used these items to wash and dry their silverware. Then they passed towel, cup, and mop down to the rest of us.

After washing our silverware, we rolled it in our white napkin. Each of us had a wide strip of material embroidered with our initials. We encircled the rolled napkin with the strip and pinned it closed. We then placed the napkin-rolled silverware in the middle of the table for use at the next meal.

As the months passed, I realized that the convent had sacramentalized many of the practical matters as eating, such as the cutting of bread. That is, at some point, someone had found a way to make holy the doing of an ordinary task. As we cut that bread we were to meditate on Jesus and his five wounds or on the Trinity. Always, the convent found ways to lift our minds and hearts to God.

The obedience of dishwashing was my culpa Waterloo. A group of six did this task for a week at a time. This was, in and of itself, noisy work. Dishes clattered; metal doors clanged; tray wheels squeaked. Even more so when done in haste so as to enjoy evening recreation in the novitiate.

After each meal, six postulants or novices removed their top veils and donned aprons. As quickly and noiselessly as possible, each of the six in the group with which I worked did one of the five steps of dishwashing. Ruth raced to the dining room to gather the dirty dishes. Placing them on one of the wheeled trays, she then propelled it down the hall to our scullery.

There, Casey had filled the deep box-shaped and metal-lined sink with hot, sudsy water. Gingerly, she dipped each stack of dishes into the sink. Because the nuns had wiped their dishes clean after eating, the dinnerware needed only a few moments of soaking before being hoisted out and swiped with a rag. Casey then eased more dirty dishes into the water while Ruth wheeled the tray out the door and scuttled toward the dining room for another load.

Casey developed an enviable rhythm: turning to the tray, lifting a stack of dishes, turning back to the sink, dipping the stack into soapy water, removing the stacks, and swiping away soapy bubbles. She did this repeatedly, almost like a robotic ballet, until she'd soaked all the dishes, glasses, cups, saucers, and dessert bowls and placed them on the metal counter to the right of the sink.

Beth, the third member of our team, stacked the soaked dishes—one by one—in large, square, metal racks with four-inch sides and latticed bottoms. She then drew up the side doors of the primitive dishwasher, which we called an oven. She shoved the filled rack over the rollers. When it was boxed in, she pulled down the doors and released a side lever. Inside the oven, jets of scalding water steamed the dishes.

As with the "soaker," Beth did this repeatedly: filled racks, shoved them one by one inside the oven, pulled the lever, waited two or three minutes while hot water sprayed the rack, lifted both doors, pushed the rack out on the other side, and propelled another rack into the oven from the opposite side. Her ballet was just a little jerkier.

Joyce and I—the fourth and fifth members of our dishwashing crew—waited on the other side of the oven for a rack to come out onto the metal counter. We dragged each released rack down the counter. Our hands darted forward, lifting the dishes one by one and swiping them dry with towels that quickly became too damp to be effective. We reached and grabbed another from the pile that sat at the end of the counter.

We stacked the dried dishes onto a wheeled tray. When we'd filled it, Meryl, our sixth team member, propelled the trolley back to the dining room where she placed the dishes on the tables for use at the next meal.

Making undue noise in the convent was evidence of carelessness—a culpa matter. When explaining the obedience of dishwashing to us, the novice mistress had given us three guidelines for doing dishwashing perfectly: "No talking. No noise. No irreverence." That is, treat the dishes as if they are vessels of the altar.

With that in mind, the first time our group of six washed dishes, I stood ready at the end of the metal counter, determined to be silent and reverent and make no noise. Quiet was the order of the day. Taking great care, I lifted a plate from the rack, wiped it dry and gingerly placed it on the tray.

Aware of passing time, I wiped and stacked a second plate. Feeling rushed, I clattered it against the first. I knelt. "Mea culpa," I said. "I was noisy."

I rose. Having lost time, I grabbed another dish to wipe. I turned toward the tray and tried to place it soundlessly on the stack. It clattered. I knelt. Made culpa. Rose. Clattered. Knelt. Rose. Clattered. Knelt. Rose. Ad infinitum.

I did this for the first meal of the day. Then the second. Finally, while I wiped the supper dishes, the five other postulants, baffled by my awkward ballet, muttered, "Stop it! Just wipe the dishes! It's almost time for recreation."

At their insistence, I became a dynamo wiper. Noisy but efficient. Of course, each evening of those seven days, I made culpa in Sister Elena's office for the faults and mishaps of the past twenty-four hours. Making culpa once a day during my dishwashing week was much more efficient than trying to be quiet during that obedience.

As I strove to increase my wiping speed, I thought of the *I Love Lucy* episode I'd seen on TV before entering. In it, a tense Lucy and Ethel stood at a conveyer belt, fumbling, bumbling, trying to grab the passing candy pieces and wrap them.

I could hardly keep from laughing whenever I remembered the two of them. As they stuffed their mouths with the chocolates piling up on the conveyor belt, their cheeks ballooned like chipmunks. I couldn't eat the dishes, but I did consider flinging them out the window. The only thing that could have made Lucy's television routine funnier was making culpa.

Singing While Sorting

Each Monday and Tuesday always found the postulants and novices in the laundry ready to tackle piles of linens and clothes. The college and academy students deposited labeled towels, washcloths, sheets, and pillowcases in the laundry chutes of their residence halls. The nuns' laundry consisted of these same items plus thick cotton half-slips and skullcaps, muslin undergarments called combinations, and linen coifs and forehead bands—all initialed with the tags they'd brought with them to the motherhouse.

The laundry itself was a one-story brick building with an attached one-story barn. The main building had formerly boasted two carriages. By the time I entered, the barn area housed a number of industrial-sized washing machines and driers. The carriage area contained a large sheet mangle and two mangles used for forehead bands. The additional space was used for sorting the clean laundry.

At some point, the nuns had added an L-shaped addition to the side of the main carriage house. It contained the four mangles needed for ironing the nuns' habits as well as their slips, which were thick, cotton underskirts with a wide waist band. In this addition were other mangles used for more detailed ironing.

Another postulant—Portia—and I were sorters. Sister Elena had given us this obedience because we had both attended St. Cordelia College the year before. Thus, we knew all the students except for the incoming freshmen. When sorting, Portia and I put everything into individual boxes labeled with college, academy, and convent dorm names. During the winter, she and I aligned these boxes inside the heated carriage house.

On balmy days, however, we arranged the boxes on benches outside the laundry, resting them against its brick front wall. Above the boxes were two adjacent windows. The two forehead band mangles stood just beyond those windows so the two novices who worked those mangles could look out and see the large oak tree in the back yard of the motherhouse.

Standing on nineteenth-century cobblestones, Portia and I sorted the laundry each Monday and Tuesday after it had been washed and dried. As we sorted, I frequently glanced upward to see Sister Michael and Sister Celia as they ironed over several hundred of the heavily starched forehead bands that the novices, scholastics, and professed nuns wore as part of their headgear. The band was a double-thick triangle of linen with strings at two of the angles for tying around the head.

Sister Michael had been one year ahead of me in college. Both of us had served as class presidents and student body presidents. She always seemed perfect to me, in every way. For the three years that she and I were together in college, I'd sought her out, waylaying her in the halls, attempting to make her laugh so she'd find me memorable and think I was special. This classic example of hero worship continued—both in college and in the convent—for over a decade.

In college, both of us had worked on the newspaper. She'd written a column I inherited after she graduated and entered the convent. Reading her witty anecdotes, students had laughed. The next year, as a senior, I spun stories that seldom elicited even smiles. To me, that was proof positive that I lacked the light touch Michael displayed. This, of course, was another reason why I idolized her: she was far more gifted than I.

Now I stood outside the window where she operated the pressing mangle. As I sorted the linens and undergarments into boxes, I sang all the popular songs of the past thirty years. When I caught her eye, I'd dance to the melody, swaying while holding a stack of towels, tap-dancing while I sorted the combinations into the convent boxes. Neither silence nor obedience mattered as I acted the happy lark for Sister Michael. She gazed out the windows and grinned at my antics; I beamed back. Life was totally satisfying.

One night during recreation I told Michael I couldn't get to sleep at night because of the neighborhood children's spirited games and their shouting and laughing. "Here's what I do," she said. "Close your eyes and pull the sheet up over your head. Imagine yourself as the baby Jesus being held by Mary on the journey to Egypt."

"Jesus?"

"Yes. Mary nestles you against her breast while the donkey trots toward Egypt. She's wrapped you in her shawl. It covers your face from the stinging, windblown sand. Just let yourself feel the beat of her heart and the donkey's gait. Relax to that rocking motion."

Throughout the remainder of my years in the convent, I traveled each night with Mary and Joseph to Egypt and slept like a baby.

At some point during my first six months in the convent, the novice mistress gave those of us who'd entered in June a talk about "particular friendships." She stressed that these were unacceptable in the convent and that none of us should choose to have a particular friend.

I mulled this mandate for a day or two before knocking at her office door. When she gave permission, I entered, walked across the room, and knelt by where Sister Elena sat at her orderly desk. In the convent all the nuns—not just the postulants and novices—knelt when speaking to a superior in her office. Kneeling bespoke the desire to be obedient to whatever would be required.

"Yes, Dee?" Sister Elena said.

"I've thought about what you said about particular friendships, and I think I need to leave the convent."

"Why is that?"

"Because I have a particular friend. . . . Sister Michael. I'm not willing to give her up. So I'd best leave."

"Dee, you and Sister Michael don't have a particular friendship."

"We do. At least I do." I was certain of this.

"I know you admire her, but that's not a particular friendship."

"What are we talking about then?"

"Let's be clear first about friendship itself. In the convent, we must avoid spending all our free time with just one person."

"Why?"

"Because if we do that—just talk to one person all the time—we separate the community into them and us. You understand?" I nodded. I'd been aware of this all through grade and high school and also college.

Sister Elena continued. "What I just described is a friendship that can lead to dissension in the community. Nuns need to avoid that. It can be divisive, but not necessarily sinful."

"These particular friendships . . . whatever they are," I said, "Are they sinful?"

Looking out the window at the vineyard beyond, she sighed, took a deep breath and plunged onward. Her voice low, resolute, she said, "In the convent, the term *particular friendship* means . . . " A blush heightened her cheekbones as she took another deep breath. "It means . . . a . . . an unnatural relationship." She gazed down at her fisted hands resting on her thighs.

I could see that the words just didn't want to come out of her mouth. Moreover, I'd realized what she was talking about and so I quickly added, "In other words, a lesbian relationship."

She drew back slightly when I said the words, then peered at me over her glasses, and asked, "You know what that means?" I nodded. "What do you know?"

So I explained how I'd first met the word *lesbian*. "One night when I was a junior, some classmates who didn't want me to be elected student body president pulled a friend of mine into one of their rooms in our residence hall. Lizbeth was sort of sensitive. Kind of fragile. Well, . . . she wasn't what you'd call 'tough.'"

Now it was time for Sister Elena to nod her understanding.

"They hammered away at her, trying to get her to say that she and I were lesbians. I was passing the door—which was sort of open—I heard them shouting that word at her. And I heard her sobbing, 'Please stop. Please. It's not true. It's not.' They just kept after her. Then I heard a loud slap and Lizbeth screamed. I shoved my way in, pushed a couple of those bullies aside, and got her out of there.

"She slept in my bed that night, and I slept on the floor. The next day, we went to the dean's office. I told Sister Mary Herbert the whole story. She sent Lizbeth to the infirmary and told me to come back before supper.

"I found out later that she interviewed all the juniors who'd been part of that group and threatened to expel them the next time they broke any college rules. She grounded them for the rest of the year. They never got to leave the campus for dates, ballgames, movies. Anything. They just stayed put.

"Sister Mary Herbert also called their parents. I wasn't worried about those juniors who wanted to ruin my reputation. It was Lizbeth I worried about. She was shaking all the time. Stuttering. A day later, her parents came and took her home. I never saw her again.

"During the rest of that school year, the juniors who'd tortured her avoided me like the plague. They spent a lot of time gossiping and lying about me. In the weeks before the school year ended, many students approached me to ask if such and such were true. Sister Mary Herbert did her part to try and squelch any rumors she heard and those seven settled into sullen silence. The following year they had other things to occupy them and we got on okay.

"I hadn't understood what they were accusing me of when they tortured Lizbeth. I'd never heard the word *lesbian*. When I asked Sister Mary Herbert why being a lesbian would have kept me from being elected student body president, she explained that the Bible teaches that homosexuality is unnatural, immoral, and sinful. This was news to me. She explained that because St. Cordelia is a Catholic college, its students have to live Catholic doctrine."

Sister Elena said, "You do understand. You and Sister Michael don't spend too much time together, and you're not involved in a lesbian relationship. You're simply good friends." I nodded, and she gave me permission to rise and leave the room.

She was right. Michael and I weren't lesbians. In fact, I wasn't aware of any sexual overtones to what I felt for her. I idealized her, yes, but I had no desire to touch her or engage in sex.

That meant, of course, I wouldn't have to leave the convent. I felt relief because I wanted to stay. Life at St. Cordelia—whether praying or working—satisfied some deep longing in my heart. I embraced the routine of religious life, even as restlessness roiled within me.

A week after I entered, Sister Elena sent a group of postulants, myself among them, to the convent kitchen to peel potatoes for supper. There I met several elderly nuns who'd come to St. Cordelia Convent from Germany four decades before. These women, who prepared all our meals, made a deep impression on me. Whether kneading bread, praying in choir chapel, or darning socks, they radiated contentment.

Soon after we'd entered, Sister Elena had explained to our postulant class that one of the customs of the convent was to say "thank you" and "you're welcome" in German. Two months passed, but nothing Sister Elena said could convince me to use the unfamiliar language.

Flummoxed, and unbeknownst to me, she asked Sister Ellie, my college mentor, to visit me. This, of course, was highly unusual because she was professed while I was simply a postulant. The convent allowed no postulant or novice to speak unnecessarily with scholastics and professed nuns, all of whom had made vows. This was because they might unduly and unwittingly influence our decision about whether to make vows.

Yet one August day in that first summer, Sister Elena summoned me to her office from the common room and gave me permission to speak with Sister Ellie. We conducted our visit on the front porch of the novitiate. I thought we were both glad to be able to speak—our first time since I'd graduated in May. I was grateful for the opportunity even though I had no idea why I'd been given permission to talk with her.

Her first words explained everything. "Dee," she said, "I've learned that you refuse to speak our German phrases. Why is that?"

"I don't see the need. English is good enough for my mom and dad. It's good enough for me."

"You don't want to honor the women who came here from Germany?"

Sister Elena hadn't used that word *honor*. I thought having to use the German phrases was just a way of making religious life a little more challenging.

Sister Ellie continued: "The nuns who do all the cooking and baking for us came here when they were just teenagers—back in 1907. They answered the ads Mother Mary Dismas put in German newspaper back then, asking for candidates to enter our convent.

"They left their families, their homes, their culture, their language behind. They boarded a freighter; spoke no English; landed a continent away; crossed several states, asking help from people speaking a language they didn't know; and entered our convent. Since then they've done nothing but serve God by serving all of us."

I was beginning to see what she was getting at.

"Using these few German phrases has been our way of giving them back a little of what they left behind. It's a way of saying thank-you."

"They all speak English now," I countered, stubborn to the end.

"How would you feel if you had to go and live for the rest of your life in Germany and hear only German and then one day someone spoke English?"

Her analogy helped me appreciate the gratitude those few German phrases represented. Still the nuns had been in the United States for over forty years. Surely English sounded normal to them now. It probably made them feel one with all of us who spoke English in an American convent. This thought lessened any guilt I might feel, so I just shrugged off her question.

Then came the zinger: "Saying those words in German is good enough for Sister Claude and Sister Mary Herbert—" Here she added several more nuns who'd taught me in college. Concluding, she said, "—and those words are good enough for me, but somehow you feel they aren't good enough for you? What makes you so special?"

My arrogance withered like weeds without water. These women—highly educated, creative in their teaching and thinking, dedicated to the life they lived—had helped shape my life. I admired each of them; I wanted to be like them.

Cowed, I whispered, "Thank you." In German.

"You're welcome," she responded—in German, of course. Then she touched my shoulder lightly with one hand, smiled, and walked back to the motherhouse.

That ended my speech rebellion. Through this incident and others in the novitiate, I learned to relinquish my questioning—to trust that others knew what was best for me. From that time on, any questioning I felt was silent. Suppressed.

Both postulants and novices took classes in two of the rooms on the first floor of the novitiate. We studied several subjects, among them: *religious traditions* developed over many centuries; *vows*—what they mean and how to live them; the *Holy Rule*, which St. Benedict wrote early in the sixth century; *prayer*—how to praise God through our chant and how to make work into prayer so as to live the Benedictine motto *Ora et labora.*

Sister Elena and Sister Mary Cait, her assistant, taught these classes. Completing our assignments wasn't always easy and left little time for individual pursuits such as playing an instrument or creating art in any way.

Fran, a fellow postulant, was a gifted pianist. However, our novitiate schedule was so busy she couldn't manage more than a few minutes of daily practice. One afternoon in early winter, I stood in the first-floor hall, listening to the music she created. Suddenly the melody stopped in the middle of a crescendo. I heard a discordant sound, then nothing. Knocking, I edged open the door. She sat crying.

"What is it? What's wrong?"

"There's no time to get it right."

In her voice I heard the longing of an artist to make music, yet nothing could be done. We were postulants, getting ready to receive the habit, and then, possibly, a year later, to make vows. If we were to stay, we had to live the life as it was presented to us. She had to accept that she'd have only a limited amount of time to practice her gift. This was all part of growing into the vow of obedience.

Once a week, a monk from a nearby monastery came to the novitiate to teach us about Gregorian Chant. He did this in the recreation room, which we also called "the common room" as all of us could use it. I thought him a handsome man and began to wonder what had brought him to the monastery when he could so easily have married.

One night at recreation, while sitting with Sister Michael, Sister Goneril, and the novice mistress, I said, offhandedly, "I wonder why Father Doherty never married. Why he became a monk instead of a dad."

All three of my listeners reacted. The two novices grinned; Sister Elena glared at me, then said, "That's uncalled for."

"I just wondered."

We were supposed to practice not only custody of the eyes but of the tongue. Given my statement, I'd been indiscreet again.

"That's worldly thinking," the novice mistress said. "Go to the choir chapel and consider what you just said. Now. Think how inappropriate it was."

"But . . ."

"Now."

In the choir chapel, I thought once again about questioning. As I considered what had happened in the common room, another question presented itself: Had I implied that a man who was handsome or a woman who was beautiful would not have a vocation?

Many of the nuns had beautiful facial features. With this realization I stepped into mental quicksand: Would I have entered if I'd been attractive? I'd had a bad case of acne for many years and hadn't felt confident about dating. Would I have entered if I'd been popular with boys and had enjoyed the prospect of a serious relationship?

Other questions bogged me down: Would I be in the convent if a neighbor hadn't molested me for three months when I was in fifth grade? Had I entered because I was afraid of sex? Had Dad's drinking been the reason I'd entered?

I didn't have answers for these pesky questions. I knew only that I wanted to pray. Perhaps there had been other factors in my decision to enter. I simply didn't have the objectivity to determine that. Still, I asked myself, *Am I, as Mom said, simply trying to run away from life?*

"O Oriens"

As a child, I constantly fell, tripped, stumbled, and zigzagged my way through each day. Consequently, Mom used to mutter, straightening the chair I'd knocked over, "Anna Dolores, you're about as graceful as a bull in a china shop." This never hurt my feelings. Most often I chortled at the image of a flame-snorting bull rampaging through a shop of delicate dishware like my grandma had in her china cabinet.

Unless truly vexed, Mom refrained from mentioning male bovines and china shops to me because I'd always immediately pass "Go" and become the raging bull charging through our five-room apartment. "Whoa!" she'd say. Then she'd settle my baby brother and me on the couch and delight us with *The Story of Ferdinand.* Mom wanted me to be as contented as that little bull, who sat on his rump and smelled the flowers.

I may have searched for contentment, but I never relinquished clumsiness. Consequently, in the convent I was always making culpa for dropping bowls, banging serving trays, and tripping over my kneeler in the choir chapel. The time I got in the most trouble came about because I was trying to be helpful—in my usual forge-right-ahead-and-damn-the-torpedoes way.

In early December, to the accompaniment of oohs! and aahs! from the novices and postulants, Sister Elena set up a fir tree in the common room. That evening we decorated it with ornaments. This pleased me no end. I was lonely, and that tree brought with it the remembrance of home.

A few days later, while most of the postulants took a class I'd already taken in college, I decided the tree was thirsty and needed a drink. It stood in a bucket of sand, so I hurried down the hall to the utility room. There I found another bucket and filled it with water. After lugging it back to the common room, I proceeded to pour the water onto the sand. Humming a carol under my breath and wondering what Christmas would be like in the convent, I remained unaware that the tree had begun to tilt drunkenly toward the floor.

I added more water. With a shudder, the tree flopped onto the terrazzo floor. Ornaments shattered. Needles skittered across the terrazzo. I stood dismayed. Surely this was a culpa matter, and I'd already been in to see the novice mistress twice that morning to confess my misdemeanors. Was the afternoon to be the same? Surely, she'd weary of hearing my sad stories of tripping, dropping a bowl, losing a pin.

The thud brought Sister Elena hurrying from her office. Speechless. For. Once.

She surveyed the fallen tree, tapped her foot next to a glass shard, sent a withering glance toward the offending bucket in which water still sloshed, and said, "Dee, you're about as graceful as a bull in a china shop." I beamed, remembering Mom and her attempts to slow down my headlong rush into life.

Sister Elena ordered me to fetch a broom and more sand from the utility room. My penance for this culpa matter was to go to the choir chapel. There I was to consider my misguided enthusiasm and my tendency to rush in without even a first thought. She often sent me to the chapel for an infraction of the rule or of the convent's traditions.

I thought Sister Elena knew that it was my favorite place among the buildings and the tombstones of St. Cordelia's. I'd entered, not so much for community, but to pray. Kneeling before the marble altar, as the sun rays suffused the stained-glass windows, satisfied my heart's deepest craving.

When I returned to the novitiate from my time in the chapel, Sister Elena was in the utility closet, returning a broom. Seeing me, she said, "You prayed?"

"Yes."

"For your faults, Dee, and I hope for mine." She smiled and I knew—for sure—that she gave me always a penance that suited my soul. She was, I thought, a wise woman.

During recreation that evening, Sister Elena hauled paper and ribbon, glue and scissors, sparkles and pipe cleaners into the common room and placed them on one of the tables. From this assortment of odds and ends, we fashioned our own ornaments for a second clothing of the bare tree. To my way of thinking, the last outshone the first.

My first Advent in the convent was a revelation. As we awaited Christmas, the Scriptures we read and the prayers we chanted brought me to a growing awareness of who Jesus of Nazareth was. For the seven days preceding Christmas, we prayed the "O" antiphons at Vespers. Each of them began with one of Jesus' attributes as given in the Bible. We chanted these ancient prayerful sentences before and after chanting a much longer psalm or canticle.

I'd never before heard of the "O," or Great, Antiphons. What they expressed was so rich in meaning that I pondered the words throughout each day. My favorite of the seven became "O Oriens." The Latin for this antiphon was as follows: *O Oriens, splendor lucis aeternae, et sol justitiae: veni, et illumina sedentes in tenebris, et umbra mortis.*

The diurnal we used for prayer contained both the Latin verse and the English translations for all the psalms, readings, and prayers we chanted. The translation given for the O Oriens antiphon, was "O Dayspring, brightness of eternal Light and Sun of Justice: come and enlighten them that sit in darkness and in the shadow of death." This antiphon probably came from a prophecy of Isaiah: "The people who walked in darkness have seen a great light; those who lived in a land of deep darkness—on them light has shined."

We prayed these "O" antiphons at the darkest time of the year—December 17 to the 23—immediately before and after the winter solstice. Ever since I'd entered—for six whole months—I'd awaken with joy. I spent the day joyfully praying and doing my obediences. I went to bed feeling joy inundate my whole being. A deep contentment enfolded me.

And yet. And yet. And yet. Even with this joy, an uncertainty shadowed my belief in myself as one who followed a Rule. I longed to walk into the light of surety. That is why the Oriens antiphon spoke to me.

This desire to walk in light led to my using the Gospels for my spiritual reading each day. I wanted to know better the *Oriens*— Christ Jesus. I hoped he'd enlighten me. I hoped he'd teach me compassion, justice, mercy, and a deep commitment to living the Gospel.

The liturgy of Advent and those antiphons changed the way I viewed Christmas. I felt I'd never before known what Christmas was truly about—the birth of someone who showed us in word and deed how to be wholly human.

One of the nuns had prepared a stable scene in front of one of the choir chapel's side altars. There she'd placed statues of Mary and Joseph, the donkey and the sheep. In front of Mary was a manger lined with straw. It awaited the coming of Jesus.

Caught up in what had happened centuries before in Bethlehem, I engaged in real magical thinking: I thought that I would enter the chapel on Christmas Eve and the babe would be awaiting me.

When I did enter the choir chapel that long ago evening, a statue of the infant lay in the manger. I saw the statue, but my heart recognized true birth. That was the reality. I pledged to myself that I'd become a saint who radiated the love expressed by the smile on that babe's face. I'd live my life always with a deep love for all of creation.

After being in the convent a half year as a postulant, I received the habit and became a novice. Before the clothing ceremony, each of us who'd entered together picked three names as possibilities for what we'd be called as nuns. I picked Mariah, Shawn, and Blaine. Sister Elena nixed all three.

"You're not a fickle wind," she said about *Mariah.* "You're here to stay." She felt that *Shawn* was too masculine for my personality. *Blaine* reminded her of chilblains and ice.

I simply couldn't think of any other name that hadn't already been taken by one of the more than six hundred nuns in the convent. Consequently, I told her to give me whatever name she thought suited me. I really didn't care.

Three days after Christmas, in an ancient ceremony steeped in ritual and beauty, we eighteen postulants received the habit. One by one we knelt before the bishop. He blessed our clothing. We then went into a side room and put aside the clothes we'd worn as postulants. Several professed nuns stood by, ready to help us don what we would be wearing for the next twelve months: black serge habit, leather belt, scapular, small skullcap, coif, forehead band, and white veil. All was solemn and sacred.

Clothed in our new Benedictine habits, we new novices processed back into the sanctuary where the bishop sat in front of the altar. One by one we again knelt before him. Blessing us individually, he then bestowed on us our religious name. All of us received the first name of Mary. Added to that was another name. For time and for eternity I was to be called Sister Mary Innocence. In the days following I chose to be called simply Sister Innocence.

On December 28 each year I would celebrate those whose name I'd been given—the Holy Innocents. They were the children put to death, nearly two millennia before, by Herod in his attempt to silence the prophesied Jewish Messiah. I thought that the name given me was a promise of both death and redemption.

After celebrating that ago-old ceremony, the eighteen of us greeted our parents and walked leisurely over to the building housing the college cafeteria. There we sat with our families at eighteen rectangular tables, decorated with white cloths and bouquets of winter flowers. Happiness surged through me—not only the joy of becoming a nun but the delight in being with my parents and my brother again. The four of us were almost giddy at being together after six months apart.

We talked over one another, guffawing, telling jokes, sharing our lives—theirs at home, mine in the convent. I begged them to tell me what was happening in Washington, D.C., and around the world. That day, they were my newspaper.

At one point I told them about the names I'd originally chosen and how surprised I was by the name *Innocence*. My brother grinned and I thought what a heartthrob he was. I saw Mom and Dad glance at one another as if they knew something I didn't.

"What? What are you thinking of?" I asked.

Then they shared their own naming story.

The previous Sunday, they explained, they'd brought to the guest living room in the main convent my Christmas gifts— a long flannel nightgown and the book *Time Without Number* by the Jesuit poet Daniel Berrigan. Mom said that Sister Elena accepted the presents graciously. Then she invited Mom, Dad, and my brother to sit on the couch while she sat in an easy chair, facing them.

As we finished off the last of our beef brisket, mashed potatoes, and green beans, Mom recounted what happened next.

Sister Elena had leaned forward and said in a confiding voice, "Mrs. Ready, Dolores is having a hard time finding a name to be called as a nun. May I tell you the name I've chosen for her and see what you think of it?"

"I'd like that."

According to my brother, Sister Elena paused as if for dramatic effect. Then, with a gleam in her eye, proclaimed, "Euchareena!"

My six-foot brother then did a fair imitation of Mom's double-take. "Pardon me?" She'd said, her voice rising. She then, my brother said, glanced at Dad to see if the name made any sense to him, but he looked as confused as she felt.

My brother ran a hand over his crew-cut and said, "She looked at me next. I couldn't keep my face straight. Euchareena? Really? Where had she gotten a name like that? Mom looked at me and all I could do was shrug."

Turning back toward Sister Elena, Mom said, "Would you say it again? I'm not sure I heard it correctly."

"Euchareena."

My brother said that Sister Elena paused, seeming to wait for an enthusiastic response. When none came, she added, "I think it's the perfect name. Dolores has a special devotion to the Eucharist. Besides that, the word *Eucharist* means 'thanksgiving.' It's clear that she's filled with gratitude. What do you think?"

"I'd like to be able to pronounce it," Mom said.

As we ate our cherry pie, Dad finished the story. "Sister Elena didn't know if your mother was kidding or not. She looked at me, and when I sided with your mother, her face sort of collapsed. I told her *Euchareena* seemed too old-maidish for you."

"And I said," my brother added with an impish grin, "that the name was too hard to pronounce. We'd stutter as we said it."

"To which I added," Mom said, "that it made me think of the word *Eureka*. Every time I heard it I was going to picture a magician performing a magic trick!"

They had me giggling, and I could see those seated at the next table laughing also. "Do you see me as the magician?" I asked.

"Certainly not. What I see is a magician having just cut you in half, shouting, 'Eureka,' as you step out of the box. You're in an orange, spangled, satin costume that shows your figure. I knew I'd laugh each time I heard the name!"

"My figure, huh?"

"Yes. That habit certainly doesn't show it. Your figure has always been eye-catching: 36. 24. 36."

I could feel myself blushing, hoping the family at the next table didn't hear mom's comment. "Maybe we need to change the conversation," I whispered. I knew that Sister Elena would frown at all this. It was "inappropriate" and "indiscreet." For sure.

To guide us away from the picture of a spangled magician's assistant I thanked Mom and Dad for being honest with the novice mistress. Despite my indifference to the name I was to receive, I wouldn't have liked Euchareena. I didn't understand why Sister Elena thought *Innocence* suited me, but anything would be better than Euchareena.

A few days later, the class of novices with whom we'd spent six months made first vows. They were now scholastics. For three years they'd live their vows at the convent and out on mission. Then they'd make final vows. In early January sixteen of them left the novitiate to live in dorms on the fourth floor of the motherhouse.

Sister Michael was now a scholastic. I wouldn't be allowed to talk with her until I, too, made first vows. Grieving, I realized that being in the novitiate with her had distracted me from any difficulties I was having in the convent.

Obstinacy

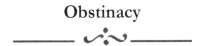

On my bedside bureau in the novitiate dorm sat a large ceramic bowl. Each night after we'd prayed Compline, I'd fill it with water. The next morning, with the curtains drawn around my cubicle, I'd sponge my body and then put on my muslin undergarment. The nuns called it a combination because like a bra it covered my chest and like a pair of panties it covered my genitalia. In fact, it covered me from shoulders to knees. The material at the top of the inner thighs was slit for ease of lavatory use. Each morning I stepped into this combination and the beige cotton underskirt that went over it. Then I began to "don my habit."

First came the habit itself—a floor-length, long-sleeved dress of seven yards of black serge. Kissing one shoulder, I quietly murmured a memorized prayer in which I beseeched God to help me live that day mindful of Graciousness. I kissed my cincture— the belt that girded my waist—and prayed again.

Finally, I kissed my scapular—a long rectangular piece of hemmed serge. It covered both the gathered front and the back of my habit. For this, too, there was a set prayer that I'd learned before the habit-clothing ceremony. I kept my folded hands under that scapular during the day so as to avoid distracting others. The only time my hands "flashed" were when I was using them to hold my diurnal at prayer, to do my obediences, or to eat.

Clothed from the neck down, I began to cover my head. First came the linen skullcap onto which I pinned the coif, or wimple, which was a large piece of pleated linen that covered my head, my entire neck, and the sides of my face. Then I tied a starched forehead band around my head. Its stiff long edge pressed into my forehead, right above my eyebrows. Next came the short, white, inner veil; and finally the long, white, outer veil. I kissed each and said a prayer appropriate to that article of clothing.

When I worked in the laundry or scullery or did other obediences that day, I'd take off the outer veil, which fell to my hips. I did this to keep it clean and out of the way. Beneath it was the diminutive white veil that came only to my shoulders. This covered my head when I worked.

Fully clothed each morning, I stood, ready for the day. I felt as if I'd donned the simplicity of Jesus. I prepared myself to follow Micah, the Hebrew Testament prophet who'd written, "What does the Lord require of you but to do justice, and to love kindness, and to walk humbly with your God?"

Throughout grade school, high school, and college, I'd memorized many poems. Most mornings, as I walked to chapel, my hands under my scapular, my eyes cast down so as not to distract others from their thoughts and prayers, I silently recited a poem by e. e. cummings. It summed up my feelings.

The following lines especially spoke to me: "i thank You God for most this amazing day . . . now the eyes of my eyes are opened."

Except for one thing, life in the convent returned to normal the day after the clothing ceremony. That one thing was a haircut. None of us had cut our hair in six months. My long hair bulged my head layered as it was with the skullcap, coif, forehead band, short veil, and long veil—all secured with a hatpin.

If someone had a cowlick, as I did, those layers of cloth could bring on a headache, and I was prone to them. Despite that, when Sister Mary Cait informed us that she'd be cutting our hair the day after the ceremony, I resisted. I'm not sure why. Perhaps sheer perverseness.

The next afternoon, after lunch, seventeen novices knocked and entered the office of the assistant novice mistress, sat down, and had their hair cut. Via one of them, I sent Sister Mary Cait the following message: "Thank you very much for offering, but I don't want a haircut."

I received a curt, no-nonsense response: "Get in here."

Shortly before we were to go to chapel to pray Matins, I ambled into her office, nonchalantly removed my headgear, and placed it on the table. After I did so, Sister Mary Cait invited me to sit down.

"Sister Innocence," she asked, "do you think you'll make first vows in a year and become a scholastic?"

"I don't know. It'll depend on whether the nuns think I have a vocation."

"I think today we have the first indicator for why they might blackball you."

"What do you mean?"

"Resisting having your hair cut doesn't bode well for taking the vow of obedience."

Oh.

"You've been headstrong. Because of that, I'll cut your hair shorter than anyone else's."

As my wavy, brunette locks fell to the floor, I said nothing, fearing the worse. When she'd finished, Sister Mary Cait directed me to stand before the mirror and look at my haircut.

While preparing myself to see a shorn head, I kept my eyes firmly closed. Then I ventured a squint. The half-inch-high hair on the top of my head stood straight up. She'd given me a crew haircut.

With my eyes opened wide, I began to smile. Broader. And still broader. For much of my life I'd thought I was adopted because no one saw any resemblance in me to other members of my family. Yet here I was with this crew cut and . . . I looked just like my brother. I wasn't adopted. Hurray and hallelujah!

My beaming face seemed to bemuse the assistant novice mistress, but before she could ask the reason for my odd response, the bell rang for Matins. I hastily reassembled the headgear, skewering it with the hatpin. "Thank you! Thank you, Sister Mary Cait!" I shouted as I rushed toward the front door.

Her parting words echoed down the hall "Remember, Sister Innocence, make culpa! You've been disobedient!"

I raced from the novitiate to the first-floor hall of the convent where I slowed down—no running in the convent or on the grounds. Still beaming, I entered the chapel just as Matins began. I'd need to kneel before the novice mistress that evening to make culpa not only for disobedience but also for being late for prayer.

This didn't faze me. If I hadn't resisted the haircut, I never would have known I wasn't adopted. Obstinacy wasn't so bad after all!

The novice mistress in any convent has a staggering obedience: She must prepare postulants and novices for the making of first vows. To do this, the candidates study the rule of the founder, his or her charism, the history of the order, and the significance of living in community. In addition, they learn the specific regulations and traditions that have attached themselves—sometimes like barnacles—to life as led in that convent.

Our class befuddled Sister Elena back in 1958 and '59. A few weeks after we'd become novices, she seemed to despair of our ever being ready to make first vows. She gathered us in the common room and told us we needed "jacking up." Our faults were many: We talked too much during times of silence. We didn't complete our work. We were noisy in chapel.

Her definition of "jacking up" meant no salutation for forty days. Forty days of silence.

During this jacking-up period, we didn't gather each evening for boisterous conversations in the common room. Instead, we sat sewing or studying without speaking. When Mother Morna Anne gave salutation in the refectory, we sat mute. We could hear the professed nuns at the other tables whispering among themselves, "What'd they do for Elena to take such extreme measures?"

After nearly a month had passed, Sister Mary Cait objected. At lunch the next day, the prioress, as usual, gave salutation to the community. The novice mistress nodded and we began to chatter. The refectory rang with our laughter.

One other time Sister Elena seemed to go overboard in her efforts to prepare us for vows. She tacked a list of faults to her office door. By each fault was the number of times she'd noticed someone being negligent. According to the list, she'd found a goodly number of straight pins on the floor. We'd dropped them and hadn't made culpa. How could we embrace poverty if we didn't lean down and pick up straight pins?

Some outlandish number of times novices had gone up the steps without holding up the skirt of their habit. This frayed the hem. Poverty again. We'd failed to close the front door quietly thus disturbing the inner peace of other nuns. The list contained a variety of other faults. All culpa matters. All with a specific number.

According to the list, we'd receive no salutation or recreation until each of us had come into her office, knelt down, and admitted our infractions. One by one, my classmates did so. Two days passed and still the list remained.

To my mind this discipline had gone on too long. The next morning, I walked into Sister Elena's office, knelt, and said, "I did everything on the list the total number of times you've indicated."

"Everything?"

"I'm at fault for all of it."

"You certainly think you're exceptional, Sister Innocence."

"I just think that pins fall without our being aware. We're young. Careless."

"True. The question is are you becoming aware of what poverty means?"

"I think so. . . . I'm trying."

"That's all I ask."

We gazed at one another. A moment of real understanding arced between us.

"Will you take down the list and accept that I did it all?" I asked.

She turned aside; I would swear she chuckled. She accompanied me out of her office and took down the list. Ultimately she came to appreciate the resilience of our class just as we came to appreciate the monumental task the prioress had given her. We were raw recruits. She shaped us into women who prayed and worked for the good of all.

The clearest example of my lack of moderation was singing as I sorted the laundry each Monday and Tuesday. Even after Sister Michael left and I had no one to impress, I continued to sing. I sorely missed dancing and singing. I missed watching musicals. Throughout my life, Mom had sung while she cooked or played solitaire or did the laundry on our wringer washing machine. I'd imitated her and did the same until entering the convent.

I'm sure Sister Elena knew I chose singing over silence each week. I didn't make culpa for this because I knew I wasn't going to stop. She never reprimanded me. The magnificence of Gregorian chant filled the lives of Benedictines. I believed she appreciated my love of singing.

One failing, however, she couldn't ignore: I was sloppy at meals. When we received salutation, I threw myself into weaving a story about the day and perhaps making the novices around me laugh. The plot, however, distracted me and inevitably I'd spill a glob of gravy on the table. Or meat juice, butter, sauce, jam, soup. So many possibilities for splotching and spotting.

When this happened, the convent required the messy person to rise, go to the front of the table, kneel, and make culpa. The penance was always the same: After the meal, I'd get a large bowl of boiling water and drape the tablecloth over it to immerse the spot. Then I'd run the edge of a spoon back and forth over it until the spot disappeared. That process, of course, made doing the laundry easier for those who did the actual washing. This was a daily occurrence for over a year.

Then, on July 11, 1959, the feast of St. Benedict, the world quaked: I got through breakfast and lunch with no spotting. In fact, I made it through the supper meat and vegetables without marring the tablecloth. Then came dessert. Poached fresh plum halves in their juice.

When the server placed the plum dessert on the table, I was telling a story about a barn swallow I'd seen fly into the laundry that morning. Intent on describing its soaring flight, I scooped one of these delicious halves from my dessert bowl. Laughter distracted me. Then . . . the splash of purple juice on white cloth.

That day of celebration had brought with it too much pure joy for me to make it through with no spotting. I rose. Walked to the head of the table. Knelt before the novice mistress. "Mea culpa, I made a plum spot on the table. If Jesus wills it, may I have a penance?"

She beamed at me. "I'm so happy to see you," she said. "It's not a feast, I've discovered, without a visit from Sister Innocence." Her words left me in a stupor. She had a sense of humor. That made all the difference in our relationship.

For me, laughter was a part of saintliness. I laughed a lot in those early months and years. In the convent, most nuns didn't consider laughter a fault except when it disturbed the silence and serenity of others. Sister Joyce, who'd entered after high school, was the novice with whom I shared a sense of the ridiculous.

We sat next to one another in chapel and across from one another in the dining room. We washed dishes and table-waited together. Often while we dried the dishes I broke out laughing at her expressive left eyebrow, raised in astonishment as I clattered and knelt like a prairie whirlwind.

She and I could bet on and giggle at the chutzpah of a grasshopper trying to bound from the mown grass to the top of the statue of Our Lady of Fatima in the side yard of the novitiate. The two of us got in trouble together because so much—whether in the choir chapel or class or laundry—tickled our funny bones. We met on the same wavelength.

In our infectious chortling in chapel and hallways, laundry and refectory, scullery and recreation, we seldom practiced any sort of moderation. We didn't simply laugh; we guffawed.

Goal: Sanctity

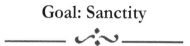

Novices served three meals a day to the community. Sister Elena divided our novice class into three crews of table-waiters. Each performed this obedience once every three weeks. The first day of table-waiting was a Sunday. On that day five of the six table-waiters began, at breakfast, to serve the nuns at the three parallel rows of tables in the refectory where they sat in the order of their entrance into the convent.

The sixth novice served the prioress and her administrative assistants who sat at the head table. I felt deep anxiety on my first day as the server for Mother Morna Anne. I'd always been so clumsy, and I feared dropping dishes or banging into the table.

With trepidation, I wheeled a squeaky serving tray down the long aisle between two of the parallel rows. Standing behind the prioress and her assistants, I reached between them to place bowls of food on the table. They passed the bowls and served themselves.

Sound engulfed the silence of that cavernous room: silverware clattered, chair legs rasped the wooden floor, and wind soughed through the multitude of open windows. Sounds from all around, but not from any of the nuns because Mother Morna Anne hadn't given salutation.

The view beyond her table diverted me. For a moment I gazed at the morning sunlight warming the courtyard cannas. Just then she cleared her throat. Startled, I snatched up the coffee pot from my serving tray, almost dropping it as my nerves jangled. I stood behind and to her side, reached down for her cup and poured the hot coffee. As my hand trembled, I placed the cup next to her right hand—without mishap. Words clamored my mind: "I've done it! I can do this! I can!"

Giddy with relief, I moved to the left and reached forward for the second nun's cup. With her wizened face, she seemed ancient to me. At twenty-three, my body was supple, my face smooth. She, slight and bent, wore wrinkles and thick glasses. I stood directly behind and to her side, held the cup near the back of her head, and began to pour her coffee. Just then, the fluty whistle of a western meadowlark beyond the open windows captured my attention. For a moment only, I forgot what I was doing. For only a moment.

That's when it happened.

I poured scalding coffee down her back.

Her yelp pierced the silence. Who would have thought that such an elderly nun could squeal so loudly? Her chair toppled over. Serving dishes teetered. Food spilled onto the pristine white tablecloth. Silverware clanked. An empty cup tumbled onto the floor and shattered. I stood poleaxed. I'd burnt a nun. I'm. Out. Of. Here. For. Sure.

The prioress immediately gave the nuns salutation. The room buzzed with astonishment over what I'd done. I wanted to run down the long aisle between the tables—my veil flapping behind me, my knees churning—and hide in one of the commercial laundry baskets beyond the mangles.

Instead, I grabbed the dishtowel hanging on the handle of my serving tray and swiped the liquid off the nun's habit. Back and forth, up and down, I swiped. The towel sprayed glistening droplets of coffee on the nuns sitting round the table.

The more I swiped, the farther away the aged nun edged to evade my fumbling hands. Despairing, I threw the damp towel on the floor, fell to my knees beside the prioress, and wailed the most heartfelt culpa I'd ever made.

Mother Morna Anne sent me to the kitchen to get rags and mops for cleaning the table and the floor. Never again did I serve her or her assistants. I was an accident waiting to happen. When I made culpa to the novice mistress that afternoon, she sent me to the college chapel to consider my faults. Her continued use of the chapel as a response to my culpas seemed, to me, to be pure gift.

During my postulancy, I'd set myself the task of becoming a saint. For me, that meant I'd be perfect in every way. I'd always resisted the urge to say or do anything unkind, critical, hurtful. In this search for perfection, I developed a renewed appreciation of observing silence. It kept me from blurting out the negative thoughts I had. Now I determined that I had to excise those thoughts from my mind. I had to be kind in thought as well as action.

When I became a novice, Sister Elena assigned me a new obedience. I was grateful for it because I thought it would help me become perfect. For the entire year I would assist the sacristan with her work in the college chapel. The professed nun who'd had this obedience for years was Sister Mary Cait —the nun who'd cut my hair.

As sacristan, she took care of the vessels of the altar—the chalice, the monstrance, the paten. She saw to the washing and ironing of the altar cloths—those that draped the altar and those used within the Eucharistic Liturgy. She darned and aired the vestments worn by the priest. In addition, she arranged elaborate vases of flowers for the main altar and the two side altars.

As her assistant, I helped prepare the altar for services. I also dusted the fourteen sculpted bronze Stations of the Cross lining the side walls of the nave and the incised marble columns that supported the altar railing. Most importantly, however, I ran a polisher on the marble floor of the sanctuary.

I'd never been particularly strong physically, but that didn't matter for this obedience. The polisher was both lightweight and efficient. Its motion—back and forth, back and forth, back and forth across the gleaming floor—mesmerized me. Peace oozed like honey through the pores of my longing for perfection.

Only then and while praying the Divine Office did I feel that I truly belonged in a Benedictine convent. In and of itself, polishing that marble floor became prayer. I felt myself descend into spiraling depths of silence. The silence of the Universe.

Sister Elena knew that I had time on my hands because the other postulants—none of them college graduates—were taking college courses I'd already passed. Somehow she knew that I enjoyed art. Thus came an obedience that lasted throughout the novitiate year: devising a new bulletin board display for each feast, season, and national holiday.

The long, rectangular bulletin board was on the wall of the corridor that led to the dishwashing room. Many of the retired nuns walked down that hall each evening after Compline. At the end of the hall were the stairs they climbed to their rooms on the third and fourth floors of the main convent building. Sister Elena wanted me to decorate the board for them.

She provided all the materials I needed: scissors, thumbtacks, glue, poster paper, construction paper, stickers, crepe paper—anything I asked for. With these, I was able to craft displays for Easter, the feast of St. Benedict, the coming of autumn, Thanksgiving, and Advent—and all the days in between.

I changed the display every two weeks or so and soon discovered that Sister Elena had been right—the older nuns did enjoy the bright colors of the bulletin board. Even though they weren't supposed to talk to a novice, they often whispered surreptitiously, "Thank you" or "Good work!" or "Beautiful," as they passed me when I was working on a new display. Their smiles lit my spirit.

Another way I got to be creative was in the use of a chisel set that Mom and Dad had given me for Christmas. The set contained three chisels of varied size. One afternoon I was sitting out in the backyard, under a gingko tree, chiseling a piece of wood to make a plaque. Suddenly, I pushed too hard; the chisel bounced off the wood and plunged into my wrist. Blood geysered upward.

Holding my arm up high, I ran toward the outside door leading into that same bulletin board corridor. I broke sacred silence by letting the screen door bang shut, but I was too scared to notice. Hurrying down the hallway to where I knew Sister Elena was meeting with the prioress, I rushed into the room without knocking.

"It won't stop bleeding," I shouted as I lowered my arm to show them. Blood gushed out of my serge sleeve and pooled on the carpet. Both Mother Morna Anne and Sister Elena gasped.

Quickly they put a tourniquet on my arm and summoned another nun to drive me to the hospital. It was the first time I'd left the convent grounds in the ten months since entering.

In Emergency, a doctor quickly assessed the problem and sewed blood vessels together. Stitching the skin of my wrist, he said, "You know, you would have achieved your purpose by driving that chisel just a little deeper and not acting so quickly."

Puzzled, I asked, "What do you mean?"

"If you want to commit suicide, you need to get a little better at this," he said, bending over my wrist.

"Suicide? I wasn't trying to commit suicide."

"Sure looks like it," he commented as he drew up the last stitch.

"Why would I commit suicide? I'm happy in the convent."

"Really?" He looked straight at me, his eyes sympathetic, his mouth curved into a gentle smile. "You don't seem too happy to me."

"Would you be if you'd cut yourself like this?"

"Fair enough," he said. "Just know that if you ever do want to get out of that convent, there are easier ways."

With that he stood up from the stool on which he'd been sitting, walked to the white divider curtain, turned back, and said, "I hope never to see you here again. Best give away that chisel set." With that he left, and a nurse gave me a pain pill.

When Sister Mary Cruz drove me back to the motherhouse, she suggested I go to the prioress's office. There, Mother Morna Anne examined my bandaged wrist and asked, "How many stitches did it take?"

After I told her, she said, "This has been quite a trauma. Go to bed and sleep through lunch and Vespers. When you wake, you can get up and come to Matins or if it's later than that . . . to supper. If you don't feel well, then just stay in bed, and I'll ask the infirmarian to come and give you another pain pill and something to eat."

Sister Elena was just as concerned and just as helpful. In a day or two the bandage came off. As time passed, the chisel cut, which looked like a crescent moon, formed a white scar.

One of the novices had found the chisel set on the ground where it had dropped from my lap when I rose and ran toward the convent. She'd wiped off the blood and put it on the chest next to my bed. It accompanied me to all the missions where I taught, but I never used it again.

St. Benedict influenced the lives of countless monks, nuns, students, and lay people throughout fifteen centuries. One reason for this was the moderation that shone through the Rule he wrote. Repeatedly, he warned against being obsessive or excessive. In hearing sentences from the Rule being read before dinner each day,

I recognized his emphasis on moderation. I don't think, however, that I ever realized that my quest for perfection was an example of being immoderate.

Each day of my novice year, I entered the college chapel and walked down its side aisle to the utility closet. I wheeled the polisher out to the sanctuary. My eyes downcast, my heart beating its hope for serenity, I began my polishing. Always I felt the tantalizing taste of sanctity. I could make myself a saint. I had no realization of the debilitating pride underlying that conviction. I actually thought God would be proud of me. As peace filled my being, I felt perfection was possible.

However, I was unable to maintain that peace once I walked through the chapel doors and re-entered the routine of my day. While I might practice outward obedience, inwardly I felt straitjacketed. Keeping custody both of my loose tongue and my judgmental mind never became easy. I never complained out loud. I simply pressed any negative feelings down into my innards where they festered.

Daily I adorned the altars. Daily I laid out the priest's vestments for the liturgy. Daily I polished. By doing so, I hoped to find salve for the festering. I hoped, too, that being in the sanctuary each day would sweeten the tartness of my tormented mind.

Through decades, thousands of young women who attended the attached college had participated in the Eucharist in that church. In the summer, the nuns teaching on various missions in neighboring states returned to the motherhouse and prayed there. All that prayer. All that graciousness. All that wholeness and holiness had left its mark.

It marked me, too, but it did not remove either my imperfections or my lack of moderation. Nor did it convince me that I should stay in the convent.

In late winter, I became more aware of loneliness; I longed for the outside world. My imperfections pressed down on me. I became obsessed with them. Two months after becoming a novice, I despaired of ever truly embracing the vow of obedience and the religious life.

One afternoon, I knocked and entered Sister Elena's office. I walked across to her desk and knelt mute for a few moments, then said, "I'm not sure I should be here. I think I need to leave the convent."

My ambivalence opened the door for her to say, "You were born to be a nun." No ifs, ands, or buts. "If you leave, you'll never be happy. In fact," she added, "you'll be miserable for the rest of your life."

Despite her insistence, I knocked at her door two more times in the following nine months, knelt, and asked if I might leave. Always she insisted that if anyone had a vocation it was I. Always she spoke of the unhappiness I'd experience out of the convent. She even said that I might go to hell.

Always she dealt with my hesitancy by sending me to the chapel to ask God to grant me certainty in my vocation. I took her at her word. She was older and wiser than I. Who was I to know what was best for me?

At lunch one day in October 1959, Sister Elena motioned for me to come to where she sat at the head of the novitiate dining table. I knelt. "Where's Sister Yvette?" she asked.

"I don't know, Sister."

"Find her."

I decided to search in the novitiate, the most likely place she'd be. More than ten months before, when I'd received the name *Innocence*, my classmate Carrie had been given the name *Yvette*. This thirteenth-century saint, who lived in Huy, Belgium, had been a wife and mother. After the death of her husband, she stayed in a leper colony for ten years, nursing those afflicted with this dreaded disease.

When Carrie and I shared the bathroom-newspaper obedience during our postulancy, we became friends. The name Sister Yvette suited the woman whom I'd learned was always willing to help anyone in need. I'd learned also that she possessed a wisdom that was part intuition and part common sense.

Entering the novitiate, I hesitated to call her name because talking wasn't allowed in the hallways. I didn't find her upstairs, but then I hadn't expected to. If she'd been sick and wanted to lie down, she'd have needed Sister Elena's permission. On the first floor I glanced into all the main rooms, hesitating before looking into Sister Elena's and Sister Mary Cait's offices. She wasn't in either room.

Putting aside the mandate of silence, I shouted her name. No answer. I shouted again, then stood silent. From the utility room came a whimper. I rushed down the hall to where we stored all the cleaning paraphernalia. Opening the door, I found Yvette huddled on the floor, trembling. Tears fell onto her dust-flaked habit.

"What is it?" I cried. "What's wrong?" I knelt, putting my arms around her shoulders. "What's happened?"

Her words coming in starts and stops, Sister Yvette said that Mother Morna Anne had called her into the convent office that morning. She'd told my friend that the convent had great hope that she'd be mother superior one day. The prioress assured her that she'd get all the training and schooling she'd need to shepherd the convent and the nuns through the years ahead.

"She can't predict the future," I muttered.

"She did . . . she said . . . she said I had a special gift. That one day . . . one, one, one day . . . I'd be mother superior."

"Tommyrot!" I insisted. "It's a bunch of tommyrot."

Yvette looked at me wonderingly. "Do you really think so? Do you really think it's tommyrot? Really? Really think so?"

"I do. No one—not even Mother Morna Anne—knows the future. She should never have burdened you with an idea that's only speculation."

"It doesn't have to happen? Does it? It doesn't does it?"

"No. Forget it. I'd like to tell Mother Morna Anne just what I think about her saying something like that to you! Life's hard enough without having that hanging over your head!"

"I can just see you telling her off!" Yvette whispered. Her words tumbled over one another, her lopsided grin at odds with the tears staining her face. I wiped away those tears with the white handkerchief all nuns carried. Together we walked back to the convent where the nuns had now gathered in the choir chapel for Vespers. We slipped into our assigned stalls, opened our diurnals, and began to pray with the community.

Yvette and I never talked about what had happened, but the incident made me question the wisdom of superiors. If Mother Morna Anne could be foolish, could Sister Elena be also? Had she been wise or foolish in saying I'd be unhappy for the rest of my life if I didn't stay in the convent?

The Benedictine vow "conversion of morals" means that a nun—walking humbly with God—will love others even when loving demands patience and perseverance. In those novitiate days, it seemed to me that no one did this more beautifully than Sister Mattie who oversaw the laundry. Each week I had the privilege of working under her patient supervision. She was, as the saying goes, as old as dirt. She had seen countless postulants and novices come and go. She knew that often we missed our families and that learning to live in community was difficult.

Deep wrinkles scored her face, mapping the peace that came from centering her life in hope and gratitude. Her voice—cracked with age, gentled by prayer—accepted everyone who crossed her path, whether we were silly or serious. Her eyes were as young and eager as a small child's. Her smile reflected the still voice of Oneness that dwelt in the deep center of her being.

Simplicity cloaked Sister Mattie. She had no axe to grind, no sorrow or shame. Each Monday, I felt she'd come to the laundry after a long visit with her God. They sat together under a white-blossomed apple tree, drinking hot coffee from chipped mugs. Together, they munched on a just-baked heel of bread and chuckled over the ups and downs of life.

As they ate, Mattie and God talked about the purity of the postulants' voices during choir practice. They shared anecdotes about the neighborhood children playing in the convent fields. They grieved together over the worrisome news of a nun whose cancer had been diagnosed the day before.

For me, Sister Mattie walked in beauty. She had looked upon the face of Jesus and rested within the deep wellspring of his love. On the days we worked, she wandered through the high-ceiled rooms, praising our work and encouraging us to take little breaks or get a drink of water. Her face held for me the promise that if I walked humbly before God, I, too, would one day radiate serenity. I'd be a saint, as she was.

Praise with Gratitude

Postulants and novices shared the obedience of delivering meals to the nuns in the infirmary. One evening in the fall of my novice year, I delivered soup to Sister Ellie, my beloved college mentor. She had heart problems. When I entered her infirmary room, she carefully edged herself into a seated position. Tenderness overwhelmed me. Casting aside the tradition of novices not speaking with professed nuns, I blurted, "You must be so holy! You suffer so much!"

"That's foolishness, Sister Innocence," she said.

"It can't be. We hear about martyrs suffering all the time. Suffering made them saints." The fact seemed indisputable to me. Suffering made saints.

"Sister Innocence, suffering in and of itself is worthless. Don't seek suffering."

"But . . ."

"No 'buts.' It's not the suffering. It's the way we respond to it."

"But . . ."

"Believe me suffering has no intrinsic value. Who would choose to suffer?"

"Well, I would if it would make me a saint."

She gazed at me with, I'm sure, a remembrance of my college days when I'd also been both spontaneous and immoderate.

"Embracing the vows you'll make will be enough," she said.

She tired then and I left her room, thinking she was just being humble. Like Sister Mattie, she was a living, walking, breathing saint. I wanted to be like her—even if that meant a weak heart or cancer.

The convent didn't emphasize pain and suffering. It was I who—after reading the lives of saints and the prophetic books of the Hebrew Testament—embraced the mistaken belief that God sent difficult situations, fatal illnesses, chronic pain, and mental anguish to those He especially loved.

Why would He do this? Easy answer: to forge them into saints. To be a saint was to suffer. That was my expectation for life as a Benedictine after making vows.

Each night as we chanted Compline, I felt gathered into the embrace of a God who was giddy with love for me. Despite my many faults, I felt this God delighted in me. Still, I wanted to present this God with a faultless human being. I welcomed the Benedictine way of life that for nearly fifteen centuries had been centered in prayer. When chanting those ancient psalms—bowing, kneeling, raising my voice in praise—I became one with all creation. Yet my embrace of the religious life was not wholehearted. I missed simple things: Stretching out on a couch. Wearing jeans. Checking out historical novels at the public library.

I missed getting a letter from my mom every week. Seeing the photographs of my college classmates' weddings and babies. I sorely missed making my own decisions about what to do with my day.

Amidst this longing for the familiar, I always returned to one truth: Prayer—with its power to soar my heart—had seized hold of me. I'd never be the same.

And so, while I laughed at the foolishness of some of the things we did and lamented my own waywardness, I continued to look forward to making vows.

One evening in mid-December, I spent my recreation time sewing nametags on the new habit and the black veil that would declare I'd taken vows for three years. I tried on new black oxfords. For several afternoons that December, the other novices and I practiced the first-vow ceremony in the college chapel.

The day after Christmas, we went on retreat. It was a time of prayer, reflection, and silence in preparation for making vows. The retreat master encouraged us to reflect on what we were about to do. He suggested we listen with ready hearts to the promptings of the Spirit within us.

While on retreat, I read *Hymns to the Church*—the Christmas gift my parents had entrusted to Sister Elena. "Prologos," the first poem in that slim volume, became my touchstone. I had hoped by this time as a religious to be well on my way to perfection, but as the poet said, I could find "no rest in my many chambers." I could not accept my own humanity.

Light through the stained-glass windows in the choir chapel colored the book lying open on my lap. The poem helped me view my convent experience within the prism of my whole life. The words that leapt from "Prologos" to my heart were these: "My love is like a stairway in the soul—but ever and forever I am only in myself." I was sure there was a clue there.

I gazed at the chapel windows. Those on one side illustrated the life of Benedict of Nursia, whom historians call the Father of Western Monasticism. Those on the other side reflected his Rule for communal living. That ancient treasure had guided the lives of innumerable women and men since he first wrote it in the early sixth century.

I hoped that Le Fort's poem and those windows might guide me through the quicksand undermining any belief I had in my vocation and myself. Her poem and Benedict's Rule prompted innumerable questions within me: *Why did you enter, Dee? What have you found here in this monastery? Is it different from what you were seeking?*

"Prologos" revealed to me that I couldn't leave myself behind no matter where I went. No longer could I deny that it was myself, not others, whom I wanted to avoid. The dark places within me were ignoble; I couldn't accept them. My only hope was that by living with so many holy women in the convent those dark places might become enlightened.

I made another important discovery during that retreat. I realized that the narrowness of my life for these many months— the physical boundaries of it and the lack of varied stimuli—had made me even more aware of what was lacking within me. Suddenly and surprisingly, I found myself wanting to take vows.

Out on mission, I'd meet students who might sing songs from Broadway musicals. I'd see the bright color of regular clothing. I'd go places in a car. Maybe just being someplace else after five hundred and forty-seven identical days would put everything in perspective. My faults and flaws wouldn't loom so large. I'd live my vows beyond the confines of the convent.

Our retreat ended with Compline on New Year's Eve. We returned to the novitiate for our final night of sleep there. Early on the wintry morning of January 1, 1960, I gazed through the frosted second-story dorm windows at the outlying stars. Who inhabited those far-flung galaxies? Did they know that here on Earth a group of novices was dressing for a day of celebration? Did the music of the spheres reach them as it did me?

I felt a singing within me. Everything—anything—seemed possible. The entire world seemed poised to welcome my vows, which committed me to this Benedictine convent. Gratitude thrummed my heart. Its beat assured me that God would accompany me on the journey I was about to take.

Soon all eighteen of us were dressed. Teeth chattering from chill and excitement, we silently left the building we'd called home for the past year and a half. We felt ready to embrace our new life as scholastics.

After Lauds and the other morning prayers, each of us stood in the foyer of the college chapel, waiting for the vow ceremony to begin. Around me, the faces of all the other novices bespoke joy. I, too, felt its sweetness and laughed aloud. Then we were all smiling, giggling, beaming, overcome with good will toward one another and all creation.

Unable to contain my happiness, I turned away from their beautiful faces to gaze through the small window facing the lawn. During the night, a blizzard of snow had fallen. Dark pine branches sagged from its weight. Beneath those trees, a few dark-eyed juncos fluttered about, fluffing their wings against the cold and imprinting spidery tracks on the snow's crest.

Suddenly, glorious music filled the chapel. We formed two parallel lines and processed down the center aisle. On each side stood the Benedictine community we were entering as well as our parents, relatives, and friends who'd gathered to celebrate with us. An unbounded smile stretched my heart. I'd made my decision. I'd chosen this life.

Now, before Mom and Dad and all the nuns at home in the convent, I'd profess, for three years, the three Benedictine vows—

obedience, conversion of morals, and stability—while embracing poverty and chastity. I was eager to make those vows. I wanted to relinquish doubt and move ahead with my life.

Large pots of poinsettias graced the high altar. Beeswax tapers, flames flaring, stood tall in gleaming candlesticks. Assembled in the sanctuary, the bishop and the clergy wore the ornate vestments of a great feast. Together all of us prayed. Sang. Knelt. A surging tide of anticipation flowed toward us from our family and friends seated in the pews. They'd come from many states to what was—for me that day—the center of the Universe.

Now came the climax of the ceremony. The bishop blessed our black veils. A professed nun moved from one novice to the next, removing the white veil we'd worn for a year. As she did so, another professed nun, standing on our other side, unfolded a black veil and covered our head with it. At the end of this solemn ritual, all of us, clothed in the black veil of the scholasticate, stood before the bishop. We lifted our palms high and joyously professed our first vows.

The ceremony ended. The pipe organ sounded its clarion message: "Te Deum Laudamus!"—"Thee, O God, we praise." That praise arched above all gathered there that day. I came new into the world.

When the rite ended, we turned and processed out into the foyer. It was there our parents greeted us. Mom and Dad hugged me. I knew they remained as unsure of my decision as I'd been. I knew also that they'd always said to me, "Dolores, you can do anything you set your mind to."

During the remainder of that day, I ate a meal with family, relatives, and friends. We then visited in the college lounge. That evening, after our guests had departed, we eighteen new scholastics prayed Compline with the rest of the community. Afterward, we climbed the stairs to the fourth floor of the convent and entered the scholasticate dorm. It was there we'd sleep for the next three years until the time came to make final vows—vows for life.

That night, lying in bed, I murmured to myself "Pied Beauty" by Gerard Manley Hopkins, one of my favorite poets. In that poem he perfectly described what the day had been for me: "With swift, slow; sweet, sour; adazzle, dim;/He fathers-forth whose beauty is past change: Praise him." I slumbered with words of praise on my lips.

Part II

The Scholasticate

Unwelcomed Surprise

The day after I made first vows, Mother Morna Anne called me into her office and explained that she'd originally planned to send me to a western state to teach. However, a sister at a mission in a neighboring state had been admitted to the hospital the day before, so for two weeks, I would take her place in a fifth-grade classroom. Then I'd travel west.

The next day, wearing my Sunday habit and the black veil of a scholastic, I traveled north. The new black leather suitcase, given to me by my parents, held my daily habit and scapular; several coifs, headbands, combinations, underskirts, nightgowns, and aprons; an extra pair of black oxfords; and my monastic diurnal and missal.

Sister Mary Nathan, who was both mission superior and school principal, met me at the train depot and drove me to the convent next to St. Joseph the Carpenter Grade School, Church, and Rectory. The next day, I began to teach. I'd taken no teaching courses, but the state allowed me to teach on the condition that I take classes in the summer and work toward certification. The fact that I'd already graduated from college helped.

When the principal and I, instead of Sister Emma, walked into the fifth-grade classroom, I saw eager faces turn puzzled. They'd last seen their teacher in December when Christmas vacation began. Now, in January, Sister Mary Nathan introduced me and explained that Sister Emma was in the hospital for a few days. Concerned, they expressed their fears about illness. The principal, her smile comforting, assured the children all would be well. Their teacher would return to them.

In the days ahead the fifth graders welcomed me, even as they missed the presence of Sister Emma. Each morning they said special prayers for her. I was eager to meet the woman who inspired such devotion and confidence. She'd left me detailed lesson plans so I'd know how to proceed and what to teach.

My one outstanding memory of that classroom is Timmy. A tall, hollow-cheeked child with sea-blue eyes and tousled chestnut hair, he sat mute in the back seat of the row next to the windows. For hours, he stared blindly ahead while lobbing a hardball into his catcher's mitt.

Throughout each of the ten days I spent in that classroom, a sorrowful river of tears flowed over Timmy's pale cheeks and plopped onto his worn jeans. His father had died in a car accident over the Christmas holidays and now his teacher was in the hospital. The children and I respected his grief and grew used to the thud, thud, thud of the ball as it hit his sweat-stained glove. Those thuds became the counterpoint to everything said in that classroom while I was there.

During recess of my final day with the fifth graders, I cheered them as they played a hilarious game of tag. They slide back and forth over the thick layer of ice glazing the blacktopped playground. Suddenly, bloodthirsty cries overshadowed our laughter.

"Kill 'im, Ben! Kill 'im!"

"Bash his head!"

"Looka' that blood!"

"Break his nose."

"Kill 'im, Ben! Kill 'im!"

"Go for his eyes!"

"Bash him a good one!"

"Kill 'im, Ben!"

The words shocked me into action. Alarmed, I rushed toward a circle of older boys gathered in the ominous shadow of the school building. They stood shoulder-to-shoulder, three deep around a center I couldn't see, shouting, punching the air with clenched fists. Oblivious to their height and bulk, I frantically tried to move them aside. None of them were familiar.

"Excuse me! Let me through. I've got to get through."

In their thick winter jackets, the boys, seemingly unaware of anything beyond what was happening in front of them, refused to budge. Their churning circle tightened. Contracted.

I shoved. Pushed. Tried to pull them apart. They shoved back. Snarled at me. Cursed. Struggling to pull them apart, I edged forward toward the center of the shouting circle.

"Keep bashin' his head, Ben! Kill 'im!"

Hearing those savage words, I instinctively looked to the left. A boy, blond hair flapping over his forehead, stared avidly at the scene before him. His body moved back and forth to the thumps coming from the center of the circle. Saliva dribbled onto his dirty white shirt. Most of its buttons had popped off so that it gaped open over his stomach, which pooched out over his tight belt.

I followed his maniacal gaze downward to where two boys struggled. One atop the other. Blood matted the hair of the one on the bottom. The boy tabled above held his opponent's head between splayed fingers. He bopped it up and down, up and down, against the ice. The boy's head thudded. Blood spurted.

The eyes of the boy on the bottom rolled back. His limp hands lay at his side.

"Kill 'im, Ben!"

The words finally galvanized me. I rushed forward; my hands gripped the shoulders of the boy doing the bopping. When I tried to pull him backward, he punched me, hitting the side of my face, barely missing my right eye. His own eyes were glazed, staring unseeingly at the presence trying to stop his crazed battering of the boy beneath him.

"It's a nun!" the boy with popping buttons shouted. "Don't hit her! You'll be excommunicated!" The shouting stopped. Silence.

The boy on top fell to the side and lay panting on the ground. The boy beneath him opened his eyes, tried to rise, fell back. Just then Sister Marie came running from around the back of the school building.

"What's happening?" she shouted.

The boy with the popped buttons tried to head her off. "Nothin's happenin', Sister. Just a friendly fight."

She stepped aside, avoiding him, and headed to where I stood, surrounded by boys, their eyes downcast. She glanced at the two struggling to get up, turned toward me, and asked, "Are you hurt?"

"He just grazed me."

"Go over to the convent and ice your cheek," Sister Marie said. "When the bell rings, I'll get the fifth-graders settled in your classroom."

As I walked away, I could hear her voice demanding an explanation from the boys. Wondering whose class it was, I felt grateful that I hadn't had to teach them for the past two weeks.

Although Sister Mary Nathan hadn't told me what time we'd be leaving for the train station the next day, I packed my suitcase Friday night, ready to go. The next morning, after prayers and breakfast, she asked me to accompany her to her office. I knelt, eager to thank her for the help she'd given me during my two weeks of teaching.

"Sister Innocence," she said, "you're staying here the rest of the school year to teach a class of seventh graders." I must have looked confused because she added, "Sister Mary Delbert who's been their teacher is being sent across the river."

Bemused, I left her office and immediately went to the basement to do my new obedience—the mission laundry. Sister Wynne, another fifth-grade teacher, came down to add an undergarment to the pile. While there, she told me that Sister Mary Delbert was finished with teaching.

"I don't understand."

"She's going to a mental facility. Didn't you see how balmy she was?"

Not only did this news totally confuse me, a nun gossiping took me aback. Repeatedly in the past eighteen months, Sister Elena had stressed we were not to gossip about others.

As Sister Wynne, who'd just ignored this tradition, ascended the steps, her final words drifted down to me like wisps of smoke from dying embers. "She trained those seventh graders like Nazi storm troopers."

On Monday morning I followed Sister Mary Nathan up to the second floor of the grade school. She pointed out her eighth-grade classroom on the left, then motioned me to the door on the right. Because someone had taped dark construction paper on the door's glass window, we couldn't see in.

Upon entering the room, Sister Mary Nathan immediately removed the paper, crumpled it into a ball, and tossed it into the wastepaper basket. Then she strode to the front of the classroom, with me following behind. Seeing me, many seventh graders nudged one another. Others rolled their eyes. Some whispered out of the sides of their mouths.

Out of those same mouths had tumbled violent words the previous Friday. They'd certainly acted like Nazi storm troopers then. I saw the boy who'd done the bopping; I saw the boy who'd lain on the ice. His shaved skull was now bandaged.

"This is Sister Innocence," Sister Mary Nathan said as I stood next to her. "She'll teach you the rest of the year."

When the boy who'd done the bopping asked where their "real" teacher was, she said simply, "She has health problems."

Sister Mary Nathan smiled at me encouragingly, then left the room, closing the door firmly behind her. She seemed confident I could do this.

Hearing the latch click shut, the seventh-graders hooted. I trembled as the volume of noise crashed around me. For eighteen months I'd known relative silence. This din hurt my ears.

"Quiet, please," I kept repeating. I could hear the plea in my voice. Bewildered, I sat down at the desk and simply gazed at them—one by one. Some fidgeted. Others fashioned spitballs and sent them spiraling toward my desk. I wiped three from my face and simply sat staring at them, saying nothing. Gradually sound hushed.

Now began the task of teaching. This was to be, I feared, a baptism by fire.

The first four weeks in that seventh-grade classroom were straight out of the 1955 movie *The Blackboard Jungle*. When I'd seen it during the summer after my first year of college, I'd thought that the unruliness and violence portrayed in the movie's inner-city classroom could happen only among those who lived in abject poverty. I didn't recognize the bias of that belief nor the naiveté.

Now, five years later, I daily entered a classroom that vied in rowdiness with the movie's. The only difference was the background of the students. Those in the movie were poor and in public high school. Mine were middle-class seventh-graders in a Catholic grade school.

Each day they entered through the door at the back of the room and dashed to their desks ready to intimidate me. My desk stood at the front of the room. As I sat there, I could look to the left of the rectangular classroom and see three rows of desks parallel to the inner wall. The twenty-eight boys sat there. To my right, along the wall of windows, sat three rows of twenty-seven girls.

After everyone had quieted on that first day, I learned that they'd completed all their textbooks before Christmas. Hearing this, my mind went into high gear. "I don't believe you know everything that's in those books," I said. "I'm going to quiz you to find out. You'll have to prove me wrong."

The challenge prompted them to take paper and pencil out of their desks with alacrity. We began: a quiz or two; recess; another quiz; lunch; another couple of quizzes; recess; a final quiz. Raucous laugher and disruption accompanied the routine. Again and again I had to stare them down.

As the day progressed, I gave a ten-question quiz on each subject area: English, geography, civics, science, reading, math, American history. Some answers required a simple true/false or yes/no; others, a word or two; still others, a paragraph of explanation. Fortunately, I'd majored in English Literature in college with minors in history, philosophy, and math. I'd had a good education. By simply paging through their textbooks, I thought of questions to ask.

After each quiz, the students traded papers. We'd discuss each question to arrive at what might seem the right answer. I insisted that we listen to other answers to the same question to determine if any of them contained some kernel of accuracy. A student could defend her or his answer when the pupil doing the grading argued with it. They seemed to love to debate, although they often resorted to put-downs and yelling. I'd remain silent, simply watching them or the clock. I seemed to befuddle them.

At the end of the day, I collected the quizzes and said I'd assign grades to them. After getting permission from Sister Mary Nathan to stay up late, I graded and then stapled together each student's quizzes.

The next day I asked Jan, one of the seventh-grade girls, to hand back the papers. She sashayed down the boys' aisles, humming. Suddenly she yelped and scurried down the row toward where I stood. Passing two other boys, she yelped again. When I asked what had happened, she smirked.

"Nothin'," she muttered. "Nothin' happened."

Walking purposefully down the aisle, amidst catcalls and hooting, I discovered that three of the boys each held a math compass. At the far end of the row sat Ben—six-foot-tall already, broad shoulders, muscled arms and chest, smug attitude. I'd recognized him as soon as I'd entered the classroom with Sister Mary Nathan on Monday morning. He was the boy who'd done the bashing on the playground the Friday before. When I stopped at the side of his desk and put my hand out for the compass, he bragged, "No girl gets by me without tasting the sharp end of my compass."

"Not anymore."

From that time on, I passed out all the papers. As I passed down the rows, the boys didn't stick a compass in my buttocks. They feared doing so. To protect herself from her own storm troopers, Sister Delbert had told them that the Church would excommunicate anyone who hurt a nun.

Chaos

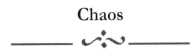

For the next four weeks I entered that classroom each day filled with anxiety, knowing that many students would refuse to listen to anything I said. All desire to dance had fled; I felt no joy. What I did feel was a tremendous need to establish order.

From the daylong quizzes I'd given on our first day together, I discovered what the students did and didn't know about each subject area. I found topics I could teach from scratch; others I could supplement.

On the second day I took from the classroom closet all the textbooks Sister Mary Delbert had collected before Christmas. I found myself puzzled: Why had she gone through them so quickly and what had she planned to do with the students for the remainder of the year?

As I distributed the books, several students pitched them through the air. They thudded against desks, chalkboards, floor, and windows. Most of the other students ducked, yelling in pain when a book hit them. I let the texts lie where they landed and tried to teach.

I began by introducing a topic from one quiz. Then I asked the students questions about it and used their answers to ask other questions. I tried to get all the students involved by relating the learning to their lives. In other words, I tried to emulate the way I'd been taught by gifted teachers throughout the years of my own schooling. A number of students—both girls and boys—paid attention. Amidst the din, they leaned forward from their desks to listen.

While many students paid attention, the others sang rowdy songs, painted their nails, practiced pitching a hardball, or styled one another's hair. Ben and his gang played poker, shouting their bets, stomping their feet, whooping. Each time the winner of a round slammed his palms down on his desk, the room seemed to shake.

Desperate by the end of the day, I sought out Sister Mary Nathan. Fearful she'd send me back to the motherhouse in disgrace—the first nun in nearly one-hundred years who didn't know how to teach—I recounted what had happened.

She listened attentively, then said, "Sister Innocence, I could come into your classroom tomorrow and take control. The thing is, as soon as I walked out, you'd lose it again. They'll even sneer at you for needing intervention."

"Then how can I get control?" I asked. "Can you help me with that? What do I do? I've never had an education course."

"A classroom like yours isn't covered in education courses," she said. "You need to figure out what works for you. Let's try to come up with some ideas."

We did that after school for four weeks, but never arrived at a strategy that worked consistently. I never asked any of the other nuns about how they handled unruly students. Quite simply, I assumed that only Sister Mary Nathan and Sister Emma had an orderly classroom. She was out of the hospital now and back on mission.

When we met, Emma welcomed me warmly. That welcome and her unfailing friendliness seemed so exceptional to me that I thought only she could discipline easily. All the other nuns, I thought, were having the same problems I was.

Because of that mistaken belief, I dreaded the future. Slowly the truth had dawned on me that if I stayed in the convent, I'd undergo this baptism by fire every September. Life would be nine months—year after year—of being a failure.

At least once a week for the first three months, a policeman visited me after school, asking questions about the students. Led by Ben, several of the boys were members of the gang terrorizing younger students in the surrounding area.

"They can bruise every part of your body and not break a bone," one young officer confided. "Every kid in this neighborhood's frightened. No one'll rat on 'em. You gotta be careful, Sister. They'll turn on ya. Right here in this classroom."

I thanked him for his advice, but I'd already learned that I needed to stay alert. That became apparent late one afternoon as I printed a tidbit of information on the chalkboard with my right hand. I heard a zing, then a thud. A gleaming knife blade, its tip embedded in the slate, quivered about an inch from my little finger. My hand started trembling.

The room was ominously silent as I turned and looked at that sea of faces. Some bore horror; others, amusement; still others, scorn. Given that the knife had come straight at my hand, I thought a boy in the row directly behind me must have flung it. I searched for a guilty look, but saw none.

My hand still trembling, I pulled out the knife and crossed the hall to Sister Mary Nathan's eighth-grade classroom room. When she came to the door, I handed her the knife and explained what had happened.

"Have all the students empty their pockets and purses on their desks. Then confiscate any weapons," she said. "I want you to stand by your classroom door each morning from now on. Have them empty out their pockets and handbags before coming into the room. Give any weapons to me."

I did this for the rest of the school year.

During those early weeks of 1960, I had one proof-positive experience of what the policeman had tried to explain to me. After school one day, David stayed to ask what he needed to study to get into college. Knowing nothing about colleges in that state, I offered to talk with the other nuns that evening and get some information for him.

The next day, I noticed that David moved as if in pain. When the other students filed out at the end of the day, I invited him to stay behind. When I asked if something had happened, he stood silent as if not sure what to say. Slowly he drew up his T-shirt. Dark bruises covered his entire chest and back. Deep purple bruises on top of bruises. Despair filled his dark eyes.

"Who did this to you?"

"The guys. In the gang."

"Why?"

"When I stayed after school yesterday to ask about college, they thought I was snitching on them. When I left here and got around the corner, they ganged up on me."

"Will you tell this to the police?"

He shook his head vehemently. "That'd land me in the hospital. Ben won't be so easy on me next time."

And that was that. I was powerless to help him.

Other students besides David also wanted to learn. Each weekday, the seventh graders and I would say our morning prayers and recite the pledge of allegiance to the flag. Then I'd begin to teach. Several students—a dozen or so—would shout, sing, curse, and yell across the room, ignoring me. They refused to open their textbooks. The others, however, leaned forward at their desks, attempting to hear my voice over the din

I thought the students might have a lot to write about. Maybe in writing they'd discover more to themselves than intimidation. That's why I made the decision to concentrate on teaching English grammar and creative writing.

We began with diagramming so that I could find out what the students knew about the parts of speech and their use in a sentence. As the noise grew in volume, I stood at the chalkboard, ignoring the recalcitrant dozen while writing sentences that I thought might capture their attention. After a while, they stopped their chattering, confused because their behavior apparently wasn't disturbing me.

In early February, I decided to try being pals with the seventh graders. Then maybe they'd like me. How wrong this notion was became clear at our Valentine's party. Besides bringing cupcakes, soda pop, and candy, several students also brought radios to the classroom. The party began in early afternoon. What ensued was like a Hieronymus Bosch painting.

Several students held a contest to see who could throw a frosted cupcake up to the ceiling and make it stick. The competition continued an interminable time with much raucous laughter. Soda pop fizzed on the floor and against the windows. Girls ran around the room, trying to evade the groping hands of the boys.

Next, three boys strutted to the front of the room, turned up the volume on their radios, and stretched out on the floor. They proceeded to hump, thrust, and moan to a rock-and-roll beat. I stood by my desk as they performed their obscene floor dance just a few feet from me. Fixing their eyes on me, they grinned at my discomfort.

That Friday-afternoon party was an ending for me. I knew I couldn't go back into that classroom on Monday.

That evening at recreation, Sister Emma must have noticed how tense I was. She asked the question no one else had asked: "How are things going for you?" Those words brought tears to my eyes. The whole sorry tale came pouring out.

When I'd finished my description of the past four weeks, she said, "We'll put a stop to that."

"How?"

I could see no happy ending. Sister Mary Nathan and I had talked almost every evening, but while her suggestions helped somewhat, the key to changing the dynamic in the classroom eluded me.

Emma invited me to detail all that had happened and what bothered me the most. Then she laid out the following plan: On Monday, I'd go into the classroom and announce a new beginning. I'd read a list of behavior I'd no longer tolerate.

Among the lengthy list we devised were interrupting my teaching and the responses and questions from others, jabbing with math compasses, throwing papers and books, spitting, cursing and sassing, getting up from desks and wandering around the classroom, talking without permission, and failing to do homework.

"The next thing you'll do on Monday," Sister Emma said, "is to explain a system of consequences."

She suggested that every time a student did something on the list, I'd print his or her name on the chalkboard and put a check by it. At the end of the day, anyone who had three checks had to stay after school.

When the students settled after school, I'd do a series of multiplication problems at my desk. I'd multiply a three-digit number by another three-digit number and get a product number. Then I'd summon each student individually to my desk and hand him or her a paper with the product printed at the top. Beneath that I'd put one of the three-digit numbers.

I'd tell the student to take the paper and subtract that three-digit number until he or she got an answer of zero. What I didn't explain is that the number would need to be subtracted as many times as the first three-digit number I'd used.

The student would then take the paper to his desk and begin. He or she would subtract the three-digit number from the product number and proceed to subtract that number repeatedly until arriving at zero. The student would stay after school until the problem was completed to my satisfaction.

"What I don't understand is how I'll know that he hasn't cheated to get out of detention early." I said to Sister Emma.

"When he shows you his work," she explained, "check it by multiplying your second three-digit number by 10, 20, 30, 40 . . . and so on. Those answers, sprinkled throughout the process, will always end in zero. Look for them. Most probably you won't find them because most students begin making up numbers to get to that final zero. You can show them where they're subtracting went askew and set them to working the problem again."

"This'll work?"

"Once the students discover just how long all that subtracting takes it will."

I worked a problem and saw what she meant. Then I went to Sister Mary Nathan to get permission to keep the students after school for as long as it took for them to do the subtraction correctly. I also needed permission to miss Vespers, which the nuns prayed together after the school day ended.

On Monday, I came into the seventh-grade classroom and announced the method of discipline that would set boundaries for the rest of the school year. I began with the following words: "For four weeks, I've given you so much rope you've hanged yourselves with it."

Those words helped me save face but were untrue. I'd given them no rope.

The truth was I simply didn't know how to establish classroom discipline in that milieu. To teach, I needed quiet punctuated by questions, curiosity, and discussion. Many of the seventh graders also wanted that. It was only the gang members and two girls who resisted.

To create a classroom in which the majority could learn, I had to become a tyrant. Only then could I keep the gang in line. I could only hope that the other students—those who wanted to learn—would understand.

When I explained the after-school subtraction problem to the students, several booed. They let me know that no one—absolutely no one— could keep them after school to do anything.

It was then I relayed what the principal had said: "Tell them that if they walk out and don't complete the problem, they'll be suspended for three days. If they do that a second time, they'll be expelled."

Sister Mary Nathan's eyes had twinkled as she told me this and she'd added, "That ought to do it."

When I played that trump card, several boys cursed. Hearing the curses, I turned my back on the class—fearful still that someone might throw a knife—and printed the names of those boys on the chalkboard with a checkmark after each name. Turning back toward them, I said, "That's for cursing. If you get two more checkmarks today, you'll stay after school."

They groaned but said no more.

To begin this new regime, I established a daily subject schedule. We'd pray, say the pledge of allegiance, and begin with religion. Following that, we'd study math, then reading, and so on. Before we began each subject that day, I distributed the textbooks for it and directed the students to open them to the section where I knew their knowledge was weak. As the day progressed, several boys sat like belching volcanoes ready to erupt.

By the day's end, four boys and one girl had three or more checkmarks by their names. They stayed after school and subtracted. Several times each of them tried to convince me that he or she had gotten to 0. In the first half hour, none had. They subtracted some more. The last student left the classroom over an hour after school ended. Fortunately, all five lived close by and could walk safely home.

Thus began the reign of Sister Innocence, tyrant.

Subtraction Discipline

For the next two or three weeks, five or more students worked on subtractions problems after school each day. As time passed, however, I added fewer and fewer checkmarks to the chalkboard. For two weeks, Ben refused to comply; Charlie and Hank looked to him for approval, so they, too, stayed after school for most nights those first two weeks after I'd initiated this disciplinary process.

Once Ben decided he'd had enough of this, he settled into brooding silence—like Heathcliff on the moors. Somewhat infrequently he'd offer an answer in class, and I'd see that he had a good brain. When I complimented him on something he'd done or said, he seemed appreciative. Because I refused to be bullied, Ben seemed to develop a grudging respect for me.

Surprisingly, until mid-March, no parents objected to my draconian rule of the seventh-grade classroom. It was then a couple came to the convent demanding that I change their daughter's grades. For the first two quarters of the school year Laura had gotten straight A's.

Because she'd done sloppy and incomplete work and scorned every assignment I gave, I gave her B's and C's. Even though she was the ringleader of the few girls who actively rebelled, she didn't get checkmarks. She was too savvy for that. Her resistance came in the way she insolently asked a question or answered one.

Laura's parents simply couldn't understand why her grades had gone down. They insisted I had a grudge against their daughter because she was smarter than I pretended to be. When I described her attitude, they maintained their daughter was smarter, more attractive, more charming than any other student in the seventh grade. Because of that, they thought, she should be given A's.

I assured Laura's parents that if her work and attitude changed for the final quarter, she'd make better grades. They left angry, but they must have spoken to their daughter because she began to respond to class questions without disdain and arrogance and she turned in excellent assignments. An attractive girl, she and Ben were a couple.

Sister Wynne had taught most of these seventh graders in her fifth-grade class two years before. Now I was teaching them. One Saturday morning, she again came to the laundry and gossiped about the past.

"You know, Sister Innocence," she confided, "that lot's not innocent. They haven't been since they started partying in the fifth grade. They changed then—and not for the better."

Seeing my befuddlement, she whispered, "Sex."

The next day I looked at those fifty-five seventh graders and felt sad for them. I could see now why several of the girls seemed too knowledgeable for their age. These same girls stood on the playground with their breasts thrust out provocatively. Most likely they had much more sexual experience than I had. That fact wasn't important. I was there to teach them; they were there to learn.

Days slipped into weeks, then months. The number of students staying after school waxed and waned. Some days a few got two checkmarks, but not three. Still, when peace became too oppressive, some boys would "act out." On the whole, however, order and balance had been established. Now I could begin to supplement the books they'd completed in the first semester.

I quickly discovered the rewards of teaching: Watching a realization dawn on a student's face. Seeing heads nod in comprehension. Listening to questions that showed critical thinking. Watching students reason. Their wanting to know more delighted me. Finding ways to the students' minds, hearts, and spirits became all-important.

During those months of teaching I developed a number of projects—some I'd been assigned when I was a student and others came from a creativity I hadn't realized I possessed. Among these projects were dioramas; debates; plays created out of the plots of books they'd read; mock radio and television news programs; soap operas; "Man on the Street" interviews; quiz shows; newspapers;

puppet shows for stories the students devised; math and science collages; and geography mobiles. These projects captured the interest of most of the students and reinforced what we were studying:

In the classroom closet, I'd discovered a large roll of newsprint that gave me the idea for a project that would involve all the students for several weeks. To begin, I asked the students to bring to class the newspaper delivered at their homes. We then scrutinized the papers. We discussed the difference between feature articles and news. We read opinions, editorials, and the letters to the editor.

The students discovered that a paper contained a wealth of information: features on celebrities, books, business, gardening, and sports; news stories; comics; obituaries; advice columns; movie reviews; weather reports; crossword puzzles.

After they'd become familiar with the innards of a newspaper, I showed them a large sheet of newsprint. We'd been studying the American Revolution, its leaders, its causes, its battles. After briefly summing up all we'd covered in our studies, I asked, "What do you think the colonists and Tories read in their newspapers?" The students responded with great enthusiasm and came up with a slew of ideas.

Next I gave each student a sheet of newsprint and encouraged the students to use their sheet to create individual two-page newspapers on the years of the American Revolutionary War. Most of the students wholeheartedly engaged in this project, which lasted several weeks and involved considerable research, writing, and creativity.

For example, they came up with letters from colonists—rebels and Tories. One student even pasted onto his paper a mock letter from King George III bemoaning the waywardness of the Massachusetts colonists and praising John Adams for defending the British soldiers who'd been involved in what Paul Revere—the master propagandist—was calling "The Boston Massacre."

When the students completed the project—on which they'd worked at home and at school—we had fifty-five two-page newspapers. The names they'd given to their various newspapers, which represented all the colonies in 1776, displayed real creativity, as did the news, features, puzzles, comics, sketches, and other writing they pasted in the columns of their papers. We thumb-tacked and taped the newspapers all around the room so the students could read and enjoy one another's work.

From mid-February to the end of the school year, I was perhaps more creative in my teaching than in any subsequent year. The passivity and boredom of some of the students challenged me.

Most of the seventh graders wanted to learn, but surely not in such a tense atmosphere. The situation was tricky for them. If they acted as if they liked to learn, the ruling gang members might await them after school and batter them into submission. If they complied with the gang's commands, then they'd likely get checkmarks on the chalkboard, stay after school, and have to answer to their parents. Yet despite the pervading fear, most students took part in discussions, followed directions, and responded well to the varied techniques I made use of to teach.

One of those students was Megan. On an April day, when no one got three checkmarks on the chalkboard, she stayed after school to ask me about college. A bright thirteen-year-old, she wanted to learn purely for the sake of learning. From my first day in that classroom, she'd paid attention and responded to questions and prompts.

The next day, Megan had a pained look on her face throughout our lessons. I discovered why only when the students filed out of the room at the end of the day. As Megan passed me, I noticed that countless dark specks marred the back of her white blouse. I asked her to step out of the line. The other students left the building while I spoke with Megan.

Sobbing, she stammered her story: She'd sat down that morning and Jan, who sat behind her in the third row from the windows, leaned forward and whispered, "I'm going to get you good for tattling."

Throughout that long school day, Jan jabbed Megan's back repeatedly with a straight pin. The dark dots were the blood she'd drawn. With each stab of the pin, she'd muttered into Megan's ear, "This is what happens to snitches."

Megan never again stayed after school to ask my advice about her future education. Jan, cursing Megan and me under her breath, did stay after school the next day to work the math problem. I'd spoken with Sister Mary Nathan about the incident, so I could say to Jan, with certainty, that if she ever again tortured anyone in our class, she'd be expelled.

One more bonfire doused. One more casualty of the civil war that raged in that classroom. One more student filled with loathing toward me.

Each afternoon, I'd deal with whatever problems arose that day in the classroom. Then I'd head over to the parish convent where we'd pray Vespers before supper. After eating, we sat around a long, rectangular table in the common room and visited. Some nuns sewed and talked to the person sitting next to them; others played a board or card game. Still others told stories about the amusing happenings that day with their students.

I enjoyed all this, but I really couldn't tell stories because Sister Mary Nathan had strongly suggested that I keep to myself what was happening in my seventh-grade classroom. She didn't want me to talk about the tense atmosphere there. She knew the other nuns would offer all kinds of suggestions, but she wanted me to solve this problem myself. Thus it was that while I listened to the other nuns weave their humorous stories, I said little.

In late winter, I caught a bad cold and did a lot of coughing in the common room. One evening, while sitting next to Sister Mary Hora, a fifth-grade teacher, I coughed, and she muttered. "Put your hand over your mouth when you cough! You're covering us with germs!" She paused before adding, "What are you? Some country bumpkin?"

I could feel the heat flush my face. I wanted to slide off my chair and sink to the floor beneath the table and just cower there. Invisible. I'd been raised in an unfinished house out in the country beyond a small town. When I'd gone away to college and met the other students from big cities like Chicago, New York, and Seattle, I'd felt as if I were the most unsophisticated person ever to study at St. Cordelia's. Now in the convent, someone had finally put a name to me. I was a bumpkin.

Sister Mary Hora asked, "How can you be so inconsiderate? Didn't your mother teach you anything?"

I could take her assessment of me, but I didn't want anyone, ever, to lambaste my mother. She'd been a wonderful mother in the midst of one drunken scene after another.

"My mother taught me manners," I said. "I'm the one who's forgotten them. Don't criticize her ever again!"

I don't know what more would have been said if the bell for Compline hadn't rung. It did, and immediately we all stopped talking, rose, and filed out of the room and down the hall to the chapel. We prayed and then went to our separate rooms to prepare for bed. The grand silence settled over the convent.

Something close to despair seeped through me as I lay in bed that night. Over and over I murmured the words, *"And all shall be well. And all shall be well. And all manner of things shall be exceedingly well."*

Julian of Norwich had said this mantra centuries before in her English hermitage and always it brought to me the enveloping cloud of God's presence. Feeling as if Love enfolded me, I let go of my peevishness toward Sister Mary Hora. She'd reminded me to put my hand across my mouth when I coughed.

I'd remember that . . . and I did.

Summer's Respite

At the end of that school year, I returned to the motherhouse. Exhausted, I was on the verge of a nervous breakdown. The prioress assigned me the obedience of taking a long nap every afternoon between Vespers and Matins. What Mother Mary Maude didn't know was that I'd come home to the motherhouse determined to leave.

I saw the future spread out into a long, dismal lifetime with classroom after classroom in which I had no control. I simply couldn't spend the rest of my life being tyrannical. For nine months of every year—year after year—I'd be a failure.

By tradition, the nuns at St. Cordelia's went on retreat in early June after all of them had returned from their missions in the five-state area. During that retreat I thought long and hard about my decision. I knew I couldn't emotionally—or physically—handle another year like the one I'd just experienced.

I'd lost ten pounds on mission and now weighed 108 pounds. My face was gaunt; my hipbones prominent.

After the retreat I knocked on the scholastic mistress' office door. When Sister Gladys, a tall, angular woman of grave disposition, bade me enter, I walked across to where she was seated and knelt.

"Sister Gladys," I said, "I've decided to leave the convent."

"Why is that?"

"I can't teach."

"How do you know?"

"I was in a seventh-grade classroom for the past five months, and it's just too hard. I can't do that again. I just can't."

She gazed at me. *Kindly*, I thought. My words poured out. "I made a mess of the whole thing. The children hated me, and I didn't like myself. I can't do it again. Years of that. It's too much."

Silently, she searched my face then spoke, her voice gentle. "Sister Innocence, Mother Morna Anne knew what she was asking of you. She knew how hard it would be. . . . You came through with flying colors. You're a born teacher."

"I don't understand. Why did she put me there if she knew it was so hard?" I was now on the verge of tears. "I'd never taught before. I knew nothing!"

"That's just it," she said. "If you'd taught before you'd have known the situation was impossible. You hadn't taught, so you thought you could do it . . . and you did."

"You mean all classrooms aren't like that? That I won't always have such troubles?"

"Never again I think."

"I'm still confused. Why did the prioress think I could do it?"

Smiling, she said what was apparently so obvious: "Because you'd been student body president in the college."

Rebuttal flashed across my mind: *Nonsense. This is pure nonsense. This is a perfect example of a non sequitur. I'm kneeling in cloud cuckoo land.*

I said nothing.

I suppose the puzzlement on my face prompted her next words. "Believe me, Sister Innocence, your next classroom won't be like that. It's as I said, you'll probably never have a classroom like that again."

Once again I accepted that my superiors knew better than I what was best for me. I stayed.

If only I could have spoken about the past six months with other scholastics who'd been out on mission. I could have asked them if they'd ever had such an experience and what they'd done. Perhaps they'd assure me, as Sister Gladys had, that all teaching wasn't like what I'd come to know.

If I could have talked with someone and shared the stories of those months I'd have released some of the tension, gotten rid of some of the stress. Just telling the story might have given it less of a hold on me, but we were not to talk about the past. There was to be no gossiping. No rehashing of what happened on mission. The past was to remain in the past, as if it had never happened.

Each scholastic had two habits, one we wore only on Sunday and the other on the remaining days of the week. When one was being laundered, we wore the other. Also, when we were "turning" one, we wore the other. That first summer in the scholasticate, I learned about "turning." Sister Gladys explained the process to us one Saturday morning.

To turn a habit was to make the back become the front by changing the sleeve openings, the yoke, and the frayed hem. The back of our daily habit had become shiny and threadbare from our having sat on it for two years. The long, narrow scapular of black serge we wore over the habit—back and front—covered the shine, but not the fraying of the material. Turning would keep the habit whole, not holey.

Sister Gladys explained to us, while I sat there feeling a deeper and deeper dread of this new obedience, that we would turn each of our two habits only once. When we wore one out on both the back and the front, we would return the used habit to the nun in charge of our wardrobes. She would then salvage any parts that were still in good condition—for instance, the sleeves—and use them to mend other habits.

Of course, the Sunday habit, worn only once a week plus the occasional feast day, lasted much longer than the week-day habit. When this daily habit wore out completely, we began to wear the Sunday habit as the new daily. When that occurred, we rejoiced because we got a spanking new habit for Sunday.

I knew from the start that turning was beyond my capabilities. So I panicked. I'd faced knives, but thread and needle were an entirely different matter. About fifteen years before, the sewing of an apron while in Girl Scouts had been a doleful experience.

Because of my lack of sewing skills, I asked two scholastic friends if they'd turn my week-day habit while I did their obediences. One waited on tables in the summer dining room; the other worked in the scullery. They also used a polisher on the terrazzo floors of the main hall. All that sounded like a leisurely summer picnic next to the ordeal of turning a habit.

My two friends thought they got the best of the deal. They actually liked to sew. When the scholastic mistress heard my plan, she said. "You'll turn your own habit."

"I don't like sewing," I explained.

"It's your habit, Sister Innocence. It's your duty to take care of it."

"I'm not good at sewing."

"You'll get good."

"Believe me, I can't sew no matter how much I try."

"If you don't learn how to sew, you'll never be a real woman," she said.

"I don't want to be a real woman if that means sewing."

She held up her right hand for silence. I closed my mouth. I'd taken the vow of obedience. I'd lived it out on mission for five months with an unruly group of seventh graders. Surely turning a habit couldn't be worse than that.

A few weeks later, I wasn't so sure. I had so many needle pricks in my fingers and left so many drops of blood on that black serge that my friends felt sorry for me. They worked on my habit whenever Sister Gladys wasn't looking. We were downright sneaky.

Because most of the professed nuns and scholastics were home at the motherhouse each summer, we chanted the Divine Office and celebrated the Eucharist in the college chapel. After supper, the Scholastics —there were probably around fifty of us—recreated beneath the arching branches of the backyard trees. We sat on park benches and chattered away, mostly about what we were learning in our summer classes. We'd discuss assignments and talk about the teaching methods used by the college instructors.

That summer and the next two I took education courses so as to be certified to teach in several states. I hoped to discover in those classes how to deal with students who were bullies. The courses, however, seldom dealt with establishing discipline, and when they did, the suggestions were so elementary that they didn't fit the situation I'd known.

One Sunday in late July, my parents came for their yearly visit. As we sat on a bench in front of the convent, Mom told me about the movie "The Nun's Story," which starred Audrey Hepburn. Earlier that year, Mom had seen the movie with several friends.

"Dolores, after seeing the movie my friends asked me if your convent was like that one in Belgium. It isn't, is it?"

"I haven't seen the movie, Mom. What's it about?"

She described for me Sister Luke's novitiate and early years in the convent; her going to the Belgian Congo and serving as a surgical nurse; her desire to spend her life serving others. Then Mom related Sister Luke's problems with obedience and some of the "strange" things the nuns had to do. The strictness of the order distressed her.

A few of the scenes Mom related matched what I'd experienced in the convent, but St. Benedict had stressed moderation in all things. The stories Mom told about Sister Luke's convent certainly didn't illustrate that.

"Is obedience hard for you?" Mom asked.

I hesitated, then assured her that it wasn't and that I was happy. I said nothing about the school year, mindful of Sister Elena's admonition to live in the present and not talk about the past.

Of course, I hadn't been permitted to talk with anyone in my class about the situation I'd just experienced. Moreover, because I was now home at the motherhouse, I wasn't allowed to talk with any of the professed nuns with whom I'd been on mission.

Scholastics visited with and talked to professed nuns only on the Fourth of July. On that day, the convent celebrated with special meals and the showing of a recent, popular movie. We could sit next to professed nuns in the college auditorium where the film was shown. We'd visit with them beforehand. In some ways it was like a date.

While I was a scholastic, the professed nun with whom I most wanted to visit was Sister Ellie. Throughout college, I'd hero-worshipped her, hanging onto every word she uttered in the classes she taught. For two scholasticate summers, I sat next to Sister Ellie in the dark auditorium at the college and watched a movie—not "The Nun's Story."

During the movie, I felt an excitement bordering on the sexual. Not that I wanted to kiss her or have a sexual relationship with her but that I was totally aware of sitting next to my idol. It was, perhaps, the same emotion I'd seen on the faces of young teenagers on Dick Clark's TV show "American Bandstand."

The movie ended. The auditorium lights came on, and I looked around as Sister Ellie and I walked toward the balcony door. It was then I realized that each scholastic had been sitting with someone whom she, too, idolized. All of us had older nuns who'd influenced our lives and perhaps our decision to enter the convent. I wondered if all the scholastics also felt as if they'd just been on a date. Were we all like those American Bandstand teenagers—thrilled to share an enjoyable experience with the one we idolized? The one who made us feel special? Confusion warred with pleasure as I walked with the other scholastics to our dorm.

Residue from Year One

In late August, Mother Morna Anne reassigned me to the mission where I'd encountered the seventh graders. This time, however, I taught a delightful class of eager fifth graders who soaked up learning. They were so different from the students of the spring before. Each day, as I walked from the mission convent to the school building, I imagined myself waltzing across the playground, fox-trotting to the front of the classroom, and quickstepping as I passed out the papers I'd graded the night before.

Only two things marred those idyllic and carefree days of my second year there: recess and the convent laundry.

In the first week, several eighth graders who'd been part of the seventh grade gang from the year before cornered me on the playground during recess. "You won't be smiling when we're done with ya," they said. "We're goin' rape ya 'til your ears spit blood."

Given the threat of rape, Sister Mary Nathan told me I was never to walk back to the convent alone. Another nun would always accompany me.

Most days during recess, several fifth graders gathered around me. They'd tell jokes; I'd laugh. One playground scene imprinted itself on my mind: I was talking with Sammy, a fifth grader who was all of four and a half feet tall, malnourished, his face thin, a shock of black hair over his forehead, a woeful look in his eyes. He was telling me about his little brother's "knock-knock jokes" when Chick, one of the eighth graders, strode up.

He was tall, at least six feet, and burly. He smirked, put one of his muscled hands around the back of Sammy's neck, squeezed, and lifted him off the ground. Sammy's feet dangled; panic widened his eyes.

"You bitch," Chick snarled. "We'll get you tonight!"

"Let Sammy go!"

"I suppose he's your pet. Probably likes you. Doesn't know what a bitch you are."

As Chick spoke, he squeezed tightly so that Sammy's face turned blue. His eyes rolled back.

"Drop him," I yelled from my five-foot-four height.

"Make me!" he shouted.

I slapped him.

The bully dropped Sammy, who crumpled to the ground, coughing. Rubbing his left cheek, the eighth-grader muttered some choice curses, clearly debating whether to hit me.

The white line across his cheek left by my slap shocked me, but I had no time to apologize because Sammy was struggling to get up, still gasping for breath. I knelt on the asphalt and gathered him in my arms. Looking up, I saw Chick looming over us, his fists clenched, his curses still bluing the air.

"I'm going to report you to the principal," I said.

With that, he turned away, sullen, and rejoined his buddies who'd been watching. I never knew what Sister Mary Nathan said to him, but that ended any playground forays of the eighth graders into fifth-grade territory.

The gang never raped me, but they did make life difficult in another way. One of my obediences was the weekly laundry. I'd pin a load on the line and go back inside the mission convent, only to return to the backyard and discover all the wet clothes trampled in the grass and dirt. After this had happened a few times, another nun stood guard during the laundry days.

As the year passed, I continued to enjoy being with the fifth graders whose curiosity made teaching and learning exciting, but I also continued to feel guilty about the hostility I'd incited in those gang members.

My family had always voted a straight Democratic ticket. They emphasized that the Democrats were concerned about everyone, not just the wealthy and big business. President Roosevelt was a hero to both Mom and Dad, and they'd taught me enough about Social Security and other Democratic accomplishments, that I knew I'd vote Democratic also when I turned twenty-one.

In the 1960 election, John Kennedy, the Democratic candidate, was a Catholic. I was excited because this was the first presidential election for which I was old enough to vote. On Tuesday, November 8, the fourteen of us who lived in the St. Joseph the Carpenter convent donned our thick, black capes in preparation for the trip to the polls. Sister Mary Nathan locked the door behind us and said, "Well, we're ready. Fourteen votes for Kennedy!"

Immediately, I determined to vote for Richard Nixon, the Republican candidate. I wasn't casting my vote for Nixon because I liked him or even knew much about him. No. I voted for Eisenhower's vice president out of pure stubbornness. No one was telling me how to think. My vow of obedience meant I obeyed my superior with regard to living the Holy Rule, but I was certain that vow did not apply to how I thought—or voted. No political opinion was necessary. It was just, "You can't tell me how to vote."

That second year on mission I finally learned a little about what a particular friendship—as defined by the convent—could entail. That school year, Mother Morna Anne assigned a nun a few years older than I to the mission. Mother had given Sister Elsa the obedience of determining how to use audiotapes with students. She was to set up a learning lab.

As I helped her develop teaching aids, we became friends. Then one night, during the grand silence between evening Compline and morning Lauds, she knocked at my bedroom door. Unsure, I opened it a crack.

Elsa whispered, "Let me in. We can talk."

"We're not supposed to," I said.

"Who'll know?"

"I would. . . . We both would." She edged forward. "Go back to your room," I said, closing the door.

Several days passed, and she knocked again, whispering my name. Throughout the next month or so, she repeated this several times. I never again opened the door. Nor did I report this to Sister Mary Nathan, who was the superior again that year. I wasn't sure what was happening. I had an inkling, but no proof. So I kept quiet.

Sister Elsa and I didn't talk about this during the day. She never raised the subject. That in itself made me suspect that her coming to my room was meant to be a clandestine meeting. I wasn't interested in a particular friendship. I meant to live my vows.

Little more remains to be said about my two years on mission at St. Joseph the Carpenter, except perhaps that we nuns practiced silence much of the time. While in the classroom, of course, we talked with and to the students and met parents. In the mission convent, all was different: we spoke to one another only during supper and at the evening recreation.

During those recreations, we talked only about those things that would cause no ripples. We laughed. Joked. Shared stories about the classroom. We were to live in the present. It was the present about which we talked. I missed my daily newspapers and the conversations Mom and Dad and my brother and I had enjoyed around the supper table, but I put all that aside. It was part of the past—a past nuns weren't allowed to acknowledge and share.

Despite my sporadic disquiet, I still felt God's call to serve Him by prayer and by serving others. I wanted to praise Him by giving my life over to service.

Obstinacy, Again

Memories of my first mission remain unclouded in my mind. As the saying goes, the squeaky wheel gets the oil, and the seventh graders there were surely "squeaky wheels." As such, they were unforgettable. Almost all the students I met in the following years were enthusiastic about learning—not squeaky wheels but well-tuned engines eager to take to the road.

In the fall of 1961, Mother Morna Anne assigned me to a mission—St. Philip Neri—in a farming community. The fifth-graders there were welcoming, happy to be one year older and to be moving toward junior high. Our only problem in the classroom was my inability to teach New Math.

That year, several states mandated a new way of teaching arithmetic. It was meant to give children a mathematical background that would prepare them to become scientists. The 1957 launch of the first Russian satellite—Sputnik I—had prompted a reevaluation of the way math was being taught in the United States. Scientists here feared that Russia was outdistancing the U.S. in space exploration.

New Math included topics such as algebraic inequalities, symbolic logic, and modular arithmetic. Despite the fact that I'd minored in mathematics in college, these terms were somewhat foreign to me.

In the summer of 1961, teachers throughout the country studied this new approach. For some reason Mother Morna Anne didn't sign me up for one of those classes. This may have been because of my college minor. Moreover, I was still taking basic education courses for certification.

Whatever the reason, I had to teach New Math to those studious fifth graders at St. Philip Neri Grade School . . . and it stumped me. Despite the fact that I'd always loved the beauty of math, I was unable to comprehend the concepts behind the new approach. Sister Aidan, however, was a natural.

The first day of teaching from the recently published textbooks revealed my ineptitude. During recess on that day and for several days afterward, I shared with Sister Aidan my difficulties. Concerned, she'd tell me how to proceed, what terminology to use, and how to illustrate a certain principle.

After a week of my bumbling along, Aidan kindly offered to come over to my classroom each day to teach New Math while I taught art in her classroom. She had seen the creativity my fifth-graders had displayed in an art project the first week of school. She proposed that she teach New Math for one period in my classroom while I taught art in hers. That way our students would get the best of what we were each able to do.

What the two of us failed to do, however, was to get the superior's permission to do this. We weren't trying to be devious, we simply felt this was an easy solution that would work out for everyone. Later, when our exchange was mentioned at recreation one night, Sister Regan, the principal, chided us for not seeking her approval. Thankfully, she didn't belabor the point.

Sister Aidan had been in the convent a number of years and took her vow of obedience seriously. Her not asking for permission to exchange those two classes was unusual. Perhaps she realized, even that early in the school year, that Sister Regan was disgruntled with me.

The reason for this disgruntlement lay in my stubbornness with regard to a household obedience at this new mission. As the only scholastic there, I did the laundry. The first time I descended to the basement to check out the clothes washer and drier, Sister Beda, the young nun who'd done the laundry the year before, followed me downstairs.

"Sister Innocence," she said, "be sure and iron Sister Regan's combinations."

"Why would I do that?" I asked.

The tradition at St. Cordelia's was that all the nuns wore ironed half-slips. The one-piece torso garment—the combination—remained un-ironed and wrinkled for everyone but the mother superior at the motherhouse. Her combination being ironed was a sign of the respect in which the nuns held her. For me, ironing Sister Regan's combination would be contrary to convent tradition.

Sister Beda explained: "She likes all her underwear ironed. Last year, that was my obedience."

"That's done only for Mother Morna Anne back home."

"I know that, but Sister Regan wants her combination ironed so you do it."

"No. I don't."

"You have to. She expects it."

"She's not our mother superior. I'm not doing it."

My refusal to do so didn't mean the combination wasn't ironed. Sister Beda simply continued throughout the year to come down to the laundry each week and do the ironing. My rebellion created more work for her.

I don't know if she ever told Sister Regan I'd refused to do this obedience. All I do know is that from the first week on mission, the superior seemed to cast a gimlet eye on me. As I struggled to put aside my own will, I repeatedly reminded myself that I'd freely chosen the vow of obedience. What I discovered in that farm community was that living that choice wasn't easy.

Sister Beda was probably my age or maybe a year or two older. Was she annoyed with me for making more work for her? Did she feel put upon? Maybe angry? I don't know because if she experienced any of these feelings, she never displayed them to me. She had a sunny disposition and seemed to hold no grudge, so I chose to accept her at face value.

She looked for good all around her and found it. Her laughter filled the recreation room each evening and made all of us smile broadly. She enjoyed life. Her lovely singing voice enhanced the Divine Office when we gathered to pray each day.

Something else happened in that first week I spent at St. Philip Neri's convent—something that also might explain Sister Regan's attitude toward me. On the fourth day of school, Sister Aidan, the teacher with whom I'd exchanged classes, served boiled eggs.

All my life I'd liked hard-boiled eggs. I'd take them out of their shell with my knife; pulp them with my fork; put butter, salt, and pepper on them; and gobble them up. I didn't like scrambled eggs that tasted "wet" to me or sunny-side-up eggs with runny centers or soft-boiled eggs that, when cracked, oozed yolk.

On that fourth day, when the bowl containing those eggs came down my side of the table, I eagerly spooned one out. To my chagrin, when I cracked it open, it bled yellow yolk. I put it aside, ate a slice of toast, said my silent prayer of gratitude for the food, and rose to leave for the classroom.

"Where are you going, Sister Innocence?" Sister Regan asked from the head of the table.

Daily we ate breakfast in silence except for grand celebrations such as Christmas and Easter or the feast days of St. Benedict and St. Scholastica. Today was a simple work day, so her voice startled all of us. Everyone looked up—first at her, then at me—as I responded with what seemed to me to be obvious: "I'm going to the playground so that when the bell rings I can lead the fifth graders to our room."

"You will sit down and eat your egg before you leave this room."

"Just the thought of soft-boiled eggs upsets my stomach," I stammered.

"You will sit down and eat that egg. You will eat one each and every time it is served to you. You will stop thinking about it. Don't be a drama queen. Stop drawing attention to yourself."

I sat, my stomach already roiling. Minutes passed. One by one each of the nuns left the table and exited the back door. I sat, unwilling to eat that egg. Thoughts of the fifth graders wandering the playground looking for their teacher filled my mind. Still I didn't eat the egg.

The house was hushed except for the sounds coming from the kitchen where Sister Aidan was washing the breakfast dishes. Just the thought of eating the yellow muck on my plate made me ill. Each time I dipped my spoon into the ooze, I gagged.

Finally, Sister Aidan entered the dining room. A woman of great good sense, she brooked no foolishness in her class, but her dark brown eyes were both kind and understanding. She had a wry sense of humor.

"Sister Innocence," she said. "Sister Regan's our superior and she always means what she says. You must eat that egg. You'd better do it now or you'll be late for class and have to make culpa this evening."

"I hate soft-boiled eggs. Just thinking about them turns my stomach."

"Then stop thinking and start doing. Take two pieces of bread and smear the yolk on them. Mash the white part and put it between the two slices and eat it as a sandwich. Do it quickly and get it over with."

She left the room; I proceeded to follow her advice. First I salted and peppered the egg. Then I smeared and mashed and scooped it all onto the bread. The resultant sandwich really wasn't so bad. Not nearly as good as a mashed hardboiled egg, but not bad enough to continue making a scene.

For the following nine months, I weekly made a soft-boiled-egg sandwich. Sure that the superior would not allow this if she saw me doing it, I always waited until everyone else had left the room. Clearly, I could be—and was—devious.

Sister Aidan's generosity of spirit got me through that year, never more so than that early incident with soft-boiled eggs. In the following months this warmhearted nun helped me repeatedly to get along with the superior.

For the first four years of my schooling—kindergarten through third grade—I'd missed three months of school out of every nine because of asthma. During each extended absence, I'd miss essential instruction. Often, when I returned to school, one or more of the students would belittle me for what I didn't know. From that time on, I'd been wary of two things: bullying and arrogance. I simply couldn't stay silent while others acted as if they were better or smarter than someone else.

Repeatedly that year at my second mission, I witnessed the superior's patronizing attitude. During recreation each evening, as we all gathered around a large rectangular table, she sat at its end with two other nuns who taught in high school. The superior seemed to think that these two matched her in intelligence and learning.

The three of them spent recreation talking about books and history as the rest of us—there were about a dozen of us on mission that year—chatted, crocheted, knitted, and played board games. Periodically, I'd glance toward the head of the table and note their condescending smiles and superior airs.

This repelled me, but I chose an inappropriate way to show my disapproval: I followed orders slowly. I spoke little to the superior. I refused to respond to any attempt she made to converse with me. Often I made my reluctance to follow her orders obvious. I thought I knew the Rule of St. Benedict better than this woman who must have made first vows at least twenty-five years before I did. I didn't recognize just how arrogant I was.

For Christmas that year, my parents sent me a cornhusk Madonna. She stood a little over five inches high. The artist had fashioned her body from a thick layer of cornhusks rounded into a full-length dress covered by a husk apron that tied around her waist with a bow in the back.

On her head was hair made from corn silk. A scrap of husk served as a scarf to cover her head. A thin strand of husk tied the scarf ends into a bow at the back of her neck. In her cornhusk arms, she held a baby wrapped in a husk wound around its small body with red thread. The Madonna's head tilted down toward the baby, the position of the head and the arms creating a poignant moment of tenderness.

Opening the box that held the Madonna and lifting it from the tissue paper, I felt a deep welling joy. Tears glazed my eyes. I wanted to rush upstairs to the room I shared with two other nuns and place the cornhusk Madonna on the nightstand next to the single bed in which I slept. That way, I could begin my day by opening my eyes and seeing the depth of my parents' love for me.

Commitment to poverty kept me from doing that. First, I had to ask the superior if I might keep this gift. Tradition demanded that I get permission to keep anything given to me. In the novitiate, Sister Elena had permitted me to keep a nightgown and three books of poetry my parents had given me for Christmas. So I knew that superiors did sometimes allow nuns to keep gifts. Still I hesitated and didn't knock on Sister Regan's door. The other nuns went in and came out and still I waited.

After we ate the feast Sister Aidan had prepared for us, we prayed Vespers. Then Sister Regan gave us salutation so that we might visit that afternoon with one another. The time had come. With some trepidation, I knocked on her door and entered the room. I knelt and showed her the cornhusk Madonna. She took it from me and held it on her palm.

"My, that's a lovely thing," she said. "I'd so enjoy looking at it each day if it were standing here on my desk."

Her words confounded me. I so wanted to keep that Madonna. Why should this woman—who didn't even know my parents—have it? Surely she wouldn't value the gift as much as I would.

It dawned on me then just how much I wanted to keep that Madonna. A sudden realization sharpened my brain: in wanting to possess something I was refusing to live the spirit of poverty.

Sister Regan and I barely abided one another. I did not feel as if she liked me, and I knew that down deep I really didn't like or respect her. None of that mattered in the present situation, however. Commitment is what mattered.

"Would you like to keep her?" I asked.

"I would love to," she said, smiling graciously. It was a smile I didn't trust. I'd seen that smile before as she skewered me with words at the dinner table and at recreation.

Yet who was I to judge this woman? I felt she'd judged me harshly for four months and here was I doing the same to her. I'd done the same for every day of those four months.

Refusing to be generous would have been churlish given what she had said, so I gave her the cornhusk Madonna. She was teaching me in her actions how to keep my vows. She thanked me for the gift and placed it on her desk.

"When you come to make culpa or ask for something," she said, "you'll get to see it here."

I felt some satisfaction at this thought. Surprisingly, I felt joy also. I'd been able to give the gift graciously. I'd let go, but what would I tell my mother when she asked the next summer where I'd placed the Madonna?

Immaturity

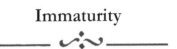

When I was out on mission each year, I'd talk with the other nuns about going home for a visit. By that, I did not mean my home with Dad and Mom. Home had become St. Cordelia's. I'd spent four college years there and was now in the fourth year of living in the convent. During the summers after taking first vows, I slept in a dorm on the fourth floor of the main convent building. Each August when nuns went on mission to the surrounding states most of them knew that they wouldn't see the motherhouse again for nine months. Distance and expense precluded their visiting.

Some missions, however, were close enough that the nuns there could drive to St. Cordelia's for an occasional Saturday visit or for a few days during Christmas vacation. During the 1961-62 school year, I was able to get home to the motherhouse once. I felt such joy in seeing several of my novitiate classmates who were either college students or out on mission as I was.

Because we were all scholastics, we got to eat at the same table. When Mother Morna Anne gave salutation, "Praise be Jesus and Mary," all of us gathered in the dining room responded, "Now and forever. Amen." Then we began to jabber. We had to be careful not to say anything negative about any other nun or about the convent and our rules and traditions. After the meal, we processed into the choir chapel and prayed together. Light shone through the stained glass windows and transformed our faces, reflecting the joy we felt to be home.

If time permitted, we walked to the cemetery. As scholastics we weren't allowed to speak to the professed nuns who had taught us in college, academy, or in our mission schools. We might smile if we saw these nuns walking in the halls or praying in chapel, but we were not permitted to speak to them. The truth was that even smiling was problematic for we would then be neglecting the tradition of maintaining custody of the eyes.

This was home and somehow when I was there, I could leave behind any unhappiness or discontent I felt. No couches or carpets or cats graced this holy place. No nooks or alcoves invited me to curl up and read newspapers. No coffee table offered novels in which I could lose myself. Despite my missing all these comforts, the convent had become home. Peace was the very air I breathed in that choir chapel and in the hallways. I felt my heart dance as I walked down those halls to pray.

And yet, ever and always, I knew I'd be going back out on mission. The other nuns seemed better able than I to accept that life wasn't perfect. I never told anyone—only Sister Elena in the novitiate and Sister Gladys during my first summer in the scholasticate—how hard I was finding life in the convent. I never spoke these words aloud to anyone else; I thought them. I thought ill of myself and of others.

"Why are we so flawed?" I asked myself again and again.

Inwardly I refused to let nuns be normal human beings. In the summers of the early 1960s, more than six hundred nuns lived at the motherhouse. I knew only a few of them from my college days and from my eighteen months in the novitiate. Still, I habitually refused to acknowledge any evidence that didn't support the romantic, unrealistic, and erroneous view I had of the convent and of religious vocations.

Sister Mary Nathan, the superior on my first mission, was everything I thought superiors always were: nonjudgmental, filled with humor, intelligent. The two "chosen" nuns and the superior on my second mission seemed the exact opposite. They were an entirely different matter. I judged them, then judged myself harshly for judging them. From that time on my mind was engaged in a battle to avoid the truth of being human.

I judged rather than simply accepted that any group of people is going to be mixed in every way. Among the many will be the compassionate and the domineering; the grateful and the embittered; the givers and the takers. In any group, we will encounter an assortment of human quirks, shortcomings, and idiosyncrasies.

The life of service these nuns had chosen might mute these human traits, but these didn't disappear with the making of vows. Living a long life in community simply smoothed the rough edges and made low the hidden valleys of traits that revealed us as flawed.

During the first weeks of being on mission with Sister Regan, I knew I was judging her and others. I got upset with myself, knowing my actions weren't those of a mature woman. In an attempt to mend and reverse my critical judgments, I found all sorts of reasons for why the superior and the nuns would act the way they did.

Rather than accept their humanity, I twisted my thoughts into a skein of knots. I made my own reality. It was only years later that I was finally able to admit that on that second mission I was seeing an example of an adolescent clique. I encountered very human behavior—behavior I refused to accept. Instead I concentrated on my own judgmental attitude and found myself despicable.

Every June the nuns went on retreat for a week. The retreat master might be a Benedictine monk or a Redemptorist or Jesuit priest. The summer of 1962, the visiting master was a tall, broad, assured Redemptorist whose clarion voice rang throughout the college chapel as we six-hundred-plus nuns listened and opened ourselves to new spiritual insights.

One day that week he spoke of particular friendships. First he described exclusive, nonsexual ones. He explained why we shouldn't select one special person above all others to befriend. In the novitiate, Sister Elena explained that by nature we might find one nun more interesting than another, but we were never to show that partiality. We were to include everyone in the welcoming friendship of our hearts and minds.

The Redemptorist reiterated this. Then he began to discuss particular friendships involving sexuality. He hammered home the established fact that they fractured the foundations of religious life, causing fissures in the community. That they led to our abandoning chastity. As he talked, I remembered Sister Elsa and the secrecy that surrounded her overtures at my bedroom door during my second year of teaching. The word *seduced* came to mind.

I'd had no problem with her being a lesbian. How other people chose to live their lives was their business, not mine. My hope was that I would always choose kindness and compassion toward others.

One of my mother's most basic beliefs was that no one should judge another's choices. "Live and let live" was a favorite saying of hers. Throughout grade and high school when I'd complain about so and so being different, acting different, looking different, she'd offered one response: "Dolores, 'Everyone to her own delight,' said Catherine O'Leary as she kissed the cow."

I wouldn't copy the Redemptorist's vigor and criticize those different from me. That decision, however, did not keep me from thinking that any woman who felt called to the religious life and made vows needed to honor her commitment to chastity. I'd come to understand that chastity was more than just refraining from sexual intimacy. A particular friendship could be an obsession with another's mind and heart. It was an intimacy of the mind. Which to me seemed just as compelling as sex.

That night, following the Redemptorist's homily on particular friendships, all of us in the scholastic dorms drew the curtains that made our single bed, two-drawer dresser, and straight-backed chair into a private cell. In the grand silence that descended upon the convent after Compline, each of us walked down the hall to the bathroom where we filled our ceramic basins with water and returned to set them on our individual dressers so we could wash our faces in the morning.

As quietly as possible, we undressed and donned our voluminous floor-length, white nightgowns. Then we pulled back the curtains so the breeze from the fourth-floor windows could sweep through the cavernous room, both long walls of which were lined with beds. A wide aisle separated the two sides.

When the lights went out, I drifted into sleep with thoughts of particular friendships. In the early morning hours, something woke me. I sat upright and looked around. The moon's rays, shining through the windows, cast shadows on the white curtains and the cream-colored walls. I saw a nun walking slowly down the aisle. She moved stealthily. Furtively.

Watching her progress down the aisle, I felt afraid. Passing the bed to the right of me, she paused at the end of my bed, turned toward me, and then reached forward and gripped my foot. I panicked.

"Stop!" I hissed. "Leave me alone!"

I was having none of this. She stepped into the space between my bed and the one to my left and walked slowly toward where I was sitting upright.

"Stop," I commanded. "Just stop it!"

She leaned over my bed. Her face neared mine. I reached up and pushed her away with a whispered shout: "Stop it!"

Her eyelids fluttering, she stammered, "What?" Then, seemingly bemused, "Where am I?"

"Not in your bed where you should be!"

She was not the professed nun from mission. She was a scholastic, and I discovered the next day that she often sleepwalked. I felt only relief. I'd begun to wonder if perhaps there was something about me that said I was interested in a particular friendship.

Because of being molested for three months when I was in the fifth grade, I'd always been afraid of sex. I wanted nothing to do with either heterosexual or homosexual relationships. Conveniently my commitment to chastity ensured I wouldn't have to deal with either.

The homily by the Redemptorist; the exchange between Sister Elena and myself about particular friendships; and the convent rules, regulations, and directives I'd studied in the novitiate class led me to a real appreciation of the wisdom of St. Benedict. His Rule had put in place safeguards to help us live in harmony with no rifts created by friendships that neglected the good of the community.

One of those safeguards was that we were not to speak to one another in the dorms or in any bedroom, be it one with a single bed or two or more. The more modern mission convents, built for that purpose, featured single rooms. My first mission convent had been built specifically for the nuns, so there I had a bedroom to myself.

However, the convent of my second mission in the farm community was a converted Victorian home in which the nuns slept in second-story bedrooms that had two or three single beds separated from one another by several feet of space.

In the convent, the prioress or mission superiors gave nuns permission to talk during lunch and supper during much of the liturgical year. However, during the six weeks of Lent and the four weeks of Advent we ate in silence. Most evenings we recreated together and the superior gave us salutation. For a span of time we'd chatter until the bell rang for Compline and the grand silence began.

This not talking during the day when we did our obediences or studied enabled us to sacramentalize what we were doing. To be present to Presence. It also did something else: it kept us from exchanging idle chatter or gossiping. In other words, friends spoke at recreation, not at other times. This, too, was a way to ensure that particular friendships didn't flourish and weren't acted on.

For the truth is that friendships that became secretive or exclusive could divide a group into "them" and "us." And that would be disruptive to the health of the community. As a group we worked together to follow the Holy Rule and serve God through work and prayer.

During one scholasticate summer, we celebrated the consecration of virgins. I found this ancient rite disturbing. A group of nuns who'd lived their final vows at least ten years processed into the sanctuary. They knelt and the priest, with loud voice and great force, uttered an anathema. That is, a curse on anyone who would violate these virgins.

At the time, it seemed to me that he ranted on and on, describing what would happen to any man who molested these women. Such a monster would go to hell. He'd burn in the eternal flames. He'd never be released from torture . . . and so on and so forth. Denunciation.

Horrified, I knelt in a pew toward the front of the chapel. No one, I thought should ever curse someone, saying that God would turn His face away from such a sinner. That God would cast that person aside. Shun him. No one had the power to do that. I did not think the Church could put into God's heart such words or intentions. I found this ceremony repugnant.

Later in the afternoon I knelt before Sister Gladys and asked if that ceremony was a requirement for being a Benedictine.

"A requirement?" she replied as if I'd uttered something truly foolish. "A requirement? It's a privilege."

"I don't ever want to be part of that ceremony. I don't want anyone cast aside because he might rape me. No one."

"Sister Innocence, . . ."

"No," I said. "If I have to go through a ceremony that would curse men I won't do it. I won't. I'll leave today."

She tried to reason with me, explaining that the religious service just showed the depth and beauty of virginity. I'd have none of it. I wanted her assurance that if I made final vows I'd never be subjected to that ceremony.

Shaking her head in what I supposed was bewilderment, she assured me that participation would be my choice. I accepted her word and left her room still bemused that the Church could permit such a curse.

I went into the chapel and meditated on violence and the response to it. By supper, my thoughts had summed themselves up into something like this: Each of us brings to our actions all the experiences of the past. For some, those experiences are tragic. Threatening. Those humans can then become beings who lash out and hurt others.

But even if those wounded made the choice to hurt others, I could not damn them. I could and probably would condemn their actions. I'd deplore their thirst for power. Their self-absorbed ignoring of the pain of another. I'd profoundly grieve that pain and the tragedies they caused. I'd abhor their violating the innocence of another person.

But I could not, would not, believe that a loving God would cast them into hell. What if they had a moment of grace? A moment of unalloyed regret for their actions? What if they accepted the consequences of their offense and felt contrition? What then? God's mercy then. Now and always.

This ruminating left me with the problem of evil. I didn't believe in devils and Satan, but I did believe in evil actions perpetrated by humans. Did I believe in evil persons? I knew about the Holocaust, about six million Jews ruthlessly murdered. Genocide. The Nazis had also starved millions of gypsies and homosexuals and sent them to gas chambers. That surely was evil.

The sexual abuse and rape of children was more than evil. I had no word for it.

Perhaps, I thought as I struggled with this question that summer, perhaps a person could do one evil act after another until at the depth of his or her being only darkness existed. Perhaps an abyss of evil. Perhaps his or her very essence became evil.

Would God damn that person if there were a moment of regret? Were some humans irredeemable? Did they even want to be redeemed? Did they want to be embraced by God's love and know the Oneness of Presence? Did such people walk the earth? If they wanted redemption, what role did I play in bringing it to them? Were we truly all One?

That ceremony of virgins led me into deep waters. Who speaks for God? What is evil? Ultimately, I found myself questioning Christianity. What was it all about anyway? With these thoughts swirling in my mind that summer, I began to examine who God was for me . . . and who I was for God. Who I wanted to be for God and for myself.

Even as I struggled with the question of evil and my own failure to become perfect, I never doubted during that summer that a benevolent God cherished me. I felt the presence of that God and knew I was a part of the Holy Oneness of All Creation.

As I walked the halls of the convent, participated in the liturgy, did my obediences, studied for my summer classes, prayed in the college chapel, ate in the refectory, walked through the cemetery, sat under a gingko tree . . . as I did everything throughout each day, I felt God's presence within me and beside me. God walked, sat, rested beside me. His presence seemed almost tangible.

I could see God smiling sympathetically as I struggled with questions that were too deep for my intellect. That God, I thought, doted on me. What else could explain the patience He had with my stumbling . . . and failing . . . again and again? He cherished me; why couldn't I cherish myself? Why did I keep judging others instead of following my mom's counsel?

Mom had said, many more times than once, "Dolores, you find what you look for. If you look for good, you will find it. And if you look for bad, you will surely find that too."

Why? Why did I keep noticing what didn't fit my definition of good? Why?

Elusive Perfection

Nuns spent at least twenty minutes each day in chapel reading from an edifying book. The convent called this "spiritual reading." The novitiate had a small library of books for this purpose; the main convent, a larger one. During my time in the convent I read a goodly number of books by Catholic theologians, biblical scholars, and spiritual writers.

Among the authors were Thomas Merton, a Trappist monk in Kentucky; Abbot Columba Marmion, an Irish Benedictine at Maredsous monastery in Belgium who had died in 1923; Jacques (French) and Raissa (Russian) Maritain, married philosophers; Jean Daniélou, a French Jesuit and theologian; Edward Schillebeeckx, a Belgian Jesuit and theologian; Bernard Haring, a German Dominican and theologian.

In addition, I read poetry. For Christmas each convent year, Mom and Dad gave me a book of poetry—three books were by the Jesuit poet Daniel Berrigan, who became an activist during the Vietnam War, and one was by the German poet Gertrude von Le Fort. Her words had influenced me during my retreat before first vows.

One day during the summer of 1962, the convent librarian approached me and asked what I was reading.

"The Bible," I told her.

"You don't have the background to interpret the Bible. You need to read biblical commentaries, but not the actual Bible."

"But . . ."

"No."

The next day she handed me a well-known commentary.

Earlier that summer, during the time set aside for spiritual reading, a professed nun in the pew behind me leaned forward and whispered, "Sister Innocence, you shouldn't be reading the Bible for spiritual reading."

I thanked her and continued reading. Perhaps she reported me to the librarian and that's why I was given a commentary. That thick volume was seldom opened. Instead, I steadfastly read all the epistles attributed to St. Paul. By the time I left the convent I'd memorized three of them: the epistles to the Philippians, the Colossians, and the Ephesians. Because of Paul's epistles, especially those three, I began to think about what made a person truly human. I longed to become the rough diamond that the vicissitudes of life faceted bit by bit into a gem of beauty.

That same summer of 1962, I realized that another nun needed me to be strong for her. She had been a close friend of mine in college. A year after I entered the convent, she graduated and also entered. That summer we were in the scholasticate together.

Throughout her life up to entering in 1959, Sister Jana had always followed her own inner intuitions and perceptions. She continued to do so in the convent. She pondered decisions; she considered what was being taught and what was being asked. She came to her decisions without haste. Not only did her mind seem to work slowly as she intuited; her body did also. She slowly moved through the halls of the convent, lumbering as she walked.

A few nuns with whom she lived on mission seemed to have little forbearance with her awkwardness. I knew that because we were on mission together for a year. The image that always came to mind when I thought of her was that of Hans Christian Andersen's ugly duckling. She appeared backward; yet she was the serene swan, inwardly dwelling in beauty.

During the celebration of the Fourth of July in 1962, she and I shared kitchen duty. After eating a celebratory supper, the nuns ambled over to the college for the annual summer movie. Sister Jana Marie and I were the last to leave the kitchen. We hung up our dishtowels, turned off the lights, and went out the side door into the evening.

I hurried down the sidewalk that connected the dining room with the administration building where the movie was being shown. Rushing ahead, I thought Jana was right behind me. I'd forgotten how slowly she walked. I'd always wondered if perhaps she lived in constant pain but simply never spoke of it.

Passing under a towering pine, I heard her voice—plaintive, pleading. "Sister Innocence, wait for me. Please wait for me."

The words shadowed my heart; they were a cry in the wilderness. In an epiphany of understanding, I realized just how hard life had been for her on mission; how little she was understood; how lonely she must be. I waited as she walked the path to where I stood under that pine. We gazed at one another—old friends. I clasped her hand.

"I'll wait," I said. "I'll always wait."

I meant that. She had become for me Jesus on the cross, crying out "Eloi, Eloi, lema sabachthani?" *My God, my God, why have you forsaken me?*

Slowly we walked together—she ungainly, I with a heavy heart—over to the main college building. The movie had already started so Sister Jana and I sat together. I had to tamp down the anger I felt toward those who were impatient with her sluggish movement and seemingly obtuse response to their questions.

If only they realized that she was the most compassionate person they might ever meet. When I was with her I felt like Moses who stood on holy ground and needed to take off his sandals and kneel. Sister Jana helped me memorize the face of God.

In June of that summer, the convent elected a new prioress—Mother Mary Maude. That fall, she sent me to a mission in a large city not too many miles distant from St. Cordelia's. Sister Mary Abram was the superior there as well as being the principal of St. Jude Catholic Grade School. A large-framed woman with a vibrant booming voice, she greeted me warmly.

"Sister Michael told me about you," she said. "I'm expecting great things."

Taken aback, I feared I'd disappoint her. As it happens I did. Three or four months after I arrived at St. Jude's, Sister Mary Abram called me into her office to tell me how disappointed she was with my failure to take hold in the classroom and engage the students.

"You're not a Sister Michael," she said.

Nothing she could have said would have made me feel worse. I'd always known I wasn't a "Sister Michael." I didn't have her ability to enliven a conversation or bring out the best in others. I wasn't a natural born leader. She was. To be compared to her so negatively was for me a moment of great shame.

My first year at St. Jude's I taught fifth grade again. As with other fifth graders I'd taught, these students were eager to learn. My only real difficulty was the teaching of science as my background in that subject was abysmal. An early chapter of the science textbook was devoted to flight. I knew nothing about the function of rudders, bracing struts, ailerons, fuselages, and other airplane body parts.

The fifth-grade boys avidly poured over the textbook pages. If only I'd known more I could have captured their attention for every subject by bringing in something about airplanes, biplanes, gliders, jets, and the whole array of planes flown at Kitty Hawk and in World Wars I and II. I could have caught their fancy with the history of nerve-racking early postal flights and barnstorming.

I could have used my own ignorance to teach. That is, I could have encouraged the students to teach me all they knew. We could have developed a unit of study that would have involved a lot of research to be followed by creative projects. None of that came about because I was too caught up in my own embarrassment to teach well. I let those students down. I was sure that Sister Michael could have, would have, done better.

Sister Mary Abram could be brusque, but she was always willing to listen to a different point of view. The only time I ever saw her be absolutely adamant about something was one afternoon in early October. The day before, Sister Sienna and I had been arranging flowers in the church sacristy when the assistant pastor, a young priest who'd recently arrived at the parish, came in from coaching football practice. The three of us began to chat about nonconsequential things that kept us laughing.

The next day, Sister Mary Abram called Sister Sienna and me into her office. As we knelt, she chided us for bad judgment: We'd been alone with a priest. This could have tempted him. We'd talked with him during afternoon silence. We'd gotten back for Vespers late.

Even as I made culpa, I didn't realize how serious this incident was.

"Your actions might affect whether or not you make final vows," she said to me after Sister Sienna had left the room to set the supper table. "Being around men . . . even priests . . . can tempt you to ignore your commitment to chastity."

With those words, I realized the magnitude of my culpa matter. From that time on I was skittish around priests.

Although Sister Mary Abram was stern about my talking with a priest, she was normally fairly easy going, making recreation in the evening enjoyable. Every Sunday evening, she surprised us with some special treat—ice cream, pie, cookies, cake, or sundaes. All of that tasted delicious because we seldom had that kind of dessert. Each Sunday it came while we sat at recreation, laughing, chatting, just relaxing before beginning the school week the next day.

Just as Sister Elena, the novice mistress, had been aware of my desire to be artistically creative, so was Sister Mary Abram. About a week before Christmas she invited me to display the Christmas village in the corner of the foyer. One side of that corner was a large plate-glass window next to the entrance door.

What a treat—to arrange the cardboard boxes for hills and valleys; to cover them with swaths of cotton so that "snow" lay on the ground; to create a village of small ceramic houses, a church, a train depot, and other buildings; to place ceramic figurines of boys, girls, men, and women throughout the village and on the hills; to place here and there the small artificial pine trees the branches of which were tipped with white paint; and finally to create a mirror lake in the middle of the village—a lake with skaters skimming over the ice.

When I'd completed the scene, Sister Mary Abram complimented me on my work. I could see that each year she delighted in this village. That to me was a sign that she was a child at heart and I found myself liking her immensely. I enjoyed the atmosphere she created at our mission.

In the nearly three years since I'd made first vows, I'd spoken with Sister Gladys, my scholastic mistress; Mother Morna Anne, and Mother Mary Maude about my hesitancy to make final vows—to vow myself for life to this Benedictine convent—on January 1,

1963. I wasn't sure I wanted to, and I was fairly certain I wasn't ready.

I deeply loved the life of prayer at the motherhouse, but out on mission our prayer was different. On some missions we prayed around a table in the recreation room. It offered no stained glass windows, altar, candles, or flowers—all of which contributed to the serenity I'd always embraced at the motherhouse.

Despite that, I enjoyed life on mission even while feeling the need to talk about the past rather than leave behind my memories. I could see the value of always living in the present—we came to one another with clean slates on which could be written the life we shared in common.

At times, all of us broke the mandate to live in the present. We shared stories from our pre-convent lives. We hummed songs that had been popular on the radio and in movies before we entered. Yes, we did slip into the past at times, then we seamlessly returned to the present and the living of St. Benedict's Rule.

It was living that Rule that would make me a saint. I was sure of that, and so it seemed to me that only in the convent was sanctity possible.

Choosing Prayer

My parents cherished me, so my childhood up to age five had been idyllic. The summer before I started kindergarten, however, they got into our Chevy with my little brother and drove away. During the next nine months they came back only for Christmas and left immediately afterward. Mom may have explained why this was happening, but I was too young to understand.

When I was older, I learned that Dad had found work in a munitions factory. In March 1941, Congress had enacted the Land-Lease Bill. The United States would ship munitions to England, Europe, and China to help them win World War II. Armament factories across the country provided countless jobs for workers who'd endured the deprivations of the Great Depression.

Consequently, they flooded the munitions' towns throughout the country. Homeowners and apartment managers had to quickly put up "No Vacancy" signs. A refurbished chicken coop was the only habitation Mom found available in the Midwestern town where Dad found work.

Years later, when I was old enough to understand, Mom explained why they didn't take me with them. "A chicken coop would have been the death of you," she said. "Before you even started school, your dad and I rushed you to the hospital six times because of asthma attacks. You nearly died four of those times."

Before they left, Mom did tell me why she was leaving me with neighbors instead of my grandmother who lived several blocks away. "Grandma can't walk you to school each day," she said. "It's too far for her."

The neighbors, however, lived right across the street from St. Alban's Grade School. "You'll be able to walk there yourself each day," Mom said. Even then she recognized that I liked to feel grown-up. I was, as my grandmother said, "an independent little Miss!"

After my family left, I missed my parents and my brother, missed what we'd done together. Now there were no Walt Disney and Gene Autry movies. No bedtime songs, porridge for breakfast, or visits to the zoo. For the first time in my life, I was without them. *What had I done? Were they ever coming back? Why did they take my brother and not me?*

Once a week during kindergarten, I had afternoon tea with my grandmother. Serving the shortbread, she invariably said, "Your shanty Irish mother made your father leave. They've abandoned you, too, Dodo."

"What does that mean, Grandma? *Abandoned?*"

"You'll never see your folks again. They're never coming back."

I didn't know what to say.

"Well? Do you want to know why?"

"Why, Grandma?"

"You're a naughty little girl and no one loves you."

Each week I'd leave her house and walk back to the Greeleys—with whom I was living. I didn't cry. Maybe crying was why my parents had left me behind. Maybe it was because I giggled. Whatever I'd done, they'd abandoned me. That's what happens to naughty little girls.

I became a solemn, quiet, unsmiling child, fearful that anything I did would make people desert me. Each day, I questioned myself: *What if my teacher doesn't like how I'm doing this? Will she tell me I can't come to school anymore? Will the other kids make fun of me?*

After I summoned the courage to do whatever a task demanded, more questions badgered me: *Did I wheeze too much? Did my school story make them laugh enough? If I smile bigger, will they like me more?*

Night and day I worried. *What if the Greeleys said, "Get out! We don't want you anymore." Where would I sleep? How would I get food to eat? What if I wore dirty clothes to kindergarten? Would the children laugh at me?*

A month before I began first grade, my parents returned. Their renewed presence in my life, however, did not change who I had become in their absence. The nine-month experience left me with a constant need to please people so they wouldn't cast me aside; it was the seed of my desire to become perfect—to become a "saint."

Throughout my years of Catholic schools, the nuns had often read aloud many stories about saints. I figured out that people admired them and God loved them. No one would cast them aside as worthless. I was sure that in the convent I could become a saint. If I made final vows, the convent would have to keep me. Forever. Never again would I be abandoned.

St. Benedict spoke not only of physical labor when he stressed the motto "Ora et Labora." Building community takes work. It takes a willingness to pray for those who annoy us. It asks us to compromise our own dream of what the convent needs to be—in our view and in our reality.

I entered the convent unaware of this. I didn't enter because I wanted to be part of a community. I wanted only to pray. Nuns did that in convents, so I entered a convent known for its life of prayer. During those first months in the novitiate, prayer enthralled me. I never doubted my reason for entering.

But as the months and years passed, inklings of the underlying reasons for my being in the convent began to gnaw away at my certitude. I wanted to pray—no doubt about that. I wanted to praise God. No doubt there either. Where wariness crept in was the reason I wanted both to pray and to praise.

Deep down in the center of my being where fear hovered, I began to remember that I'd been abandoned in the past. At six years of age, I'd concluded that abandonment happened because I wasn't perfect. Here then was my reason for being a nun: I believed that if I prayed hard enough I'd become perfect. Everyone would see me as a saint. I'd be loved unconditionally; no one would abandon me ever again.

All those thoughts of perfection and sanctity, abandonment and unworthiness, prayer and praise warred within me. As soon as I went out on mission to teach, I learned how judgmental I was. As flawed as I was, how could I ever become perfect? How could I ever be known as a saint? Each year on mission, the question became clearer to me: how could I be perfect when I harshly judged both myself and others?

The years made clear to me that nuns had to work each day to make a community out of diversity; out of a shared vision; out of a profound willingness to compromise and let go of self-absorption.

What was asked of each community member was the willingness to place the good of the whole before the doggedness of any one member of the group. Living the Rule helped bring that about. From the beginning I misunderstood the intent of monasticism. I was reluctant to embrace the rough lion's paw of communal living.

In the last months of 1962 the time came for me to decide if I could choose communal living over my own needs. I experienced a persistent battle between idealism and realism. Being the idealistic Sister Innocence, I wanted to present a perfect being to the God whom I believed had beckoned me to prayer. I simply didn't realize that God might have summoned me to live in community and that prayer cemented the community together.

The idealistic me often wore blinders. Only later did I realize that I had often been oblivious to the reality that the women with whom I lived were simply human. I refused to embrace them as they were. I found them acceptable only by wrapping them in a halo of unreality. I was unable to accept imperfection. That is, I could not accept what being human means.

Moreover, while I willingly obeyed the Holy Rule of St. Benedict, written in the sixth century, newer traditions troubled me. They often seemed foolish. This reluctance to put aside my will watered the seeds of doubt.

Despite my various misdemeanors during the three years of the scholasticate, the convent accepted me for final vows. I requested permission to make them because I couldn't bear to relinquish the life of prayer the convent offered me. The last week of December 1962, I went on final-vow retreat with the other scholastics from my entrance class. I did not enter that retreat casually. Instead I continued to ponder what I'd realized about myself and community life.

I accepted that I was a loner. Perhaps a narcissistic one. The monastic life was a life of community, not isolation. I had finally reached the point where I could no longer avoid the truth: I was unable to embrace the humanity that comes with real community.

Despite my desire for a life of solitude in which I could struggle only with my own faults and not with the foibles of others, I still made vows. I wasn't really choosing community; I was choosing prayer. While on retreat I reread and mediated on the epistles of St.

Paul and my poetry books. I listened intently to the retreat master, assuring myself that my lack of commitment to community wasn't harmful to the convent of St. Cordelia. I avoided the thought that I was offering God only half a loaf.

On January 1, 1963, I processed into the college chapel with the other scholastics who'd decided to make final vows. Seated there were our families and all the nuns who were home that day. In the sanctuary we knelt and prayed together. Then we prostrated ourselves on the cool marble floor, our arms extended.

Behind us stood four nuns, each holding a corner of a funeral pall. They laid it on top of us and placed four funeral candles in tall candlesticks at the corners. The bishop recited the funeral psalm. Incense filled the air; the chapel bells tolled out our death to the world.

In my heart I welcomed the vows I was making. I vowed to live in obedience. To live chastely. To embrace not just poverty but to let go of the desire to own anything. That is, to live within a poverty of spirit. Finally, without really understanding this commitment, I dedicated my life to building community, but in my own heart, I vowed to become a saint.

After the ceremony we newly professed nuns ate a meal with our family. My father had always been bothered by the rule that I couldn't come home for an occasional meal. Even if someone at home was dying, I had to stay at a local convent and eat my meals there.

Dad missed our dinner conversations that occurred throughout my growing up. In those conversations we'd talk about what was going on in the world beyond the United States; about politics, both local and national; about baseball and the local Class Triple A team; about the opinion and editorial columns in the newspaper. Dad missed that; I did, too.

I was keenly aware of how much he appreciated the meal we ate together that day. It was a delicious dinner served in the college cafeteria. White cloths covered the tables on each of which was a vase of fresh flowers. Sunlight streamed through the windows that made up two walls of the room. All the families of the professed nuns and the nuns themselves, myself among them, shared stories. Laughter filled the room and grew louder and louder as everyone settled into the joy of being together.

At some point that day a photographer took a picture of the newly professed. We each wore a crown of evergreen, a sign of our everlasting commitment.

After Mom and Dad left to return home, I climbed the steps to the dorm at the far end of the fourth-floor hall. In my assigned cubicle, I began to pack the leather suitcase they had given me to celebrate my profession.

As I folded my daily habit, a frisson of stark terror pierced me. Abandonment riddled my body, coursing through me. Everything was dark. A void. I could feel the sharp edges of nails piercing my hands, fastening them to a cross that hung in space. Everyone—even God—had deserted me.

I could feel desolate loneliness hardening every pore of my body. It stretched my skin to bursting so that it coursed out into the Universe, and a cry pierced the music of the spheres. My cry of abandonment. Of loneliness. Of desertion. Of utter fear.

Knowing only deep darkness, I fell to the terrazzo floor. I was in a cavern of overlapping shadows. They passed through me, like mist, piercing me like shards of isolation. Words filled my mind. Seven words. Over and over. *My God, why have you forsaken me?* The words echoed in my brain even as the shadows seared the deep hollow within me.

When I came to, I felt emptied, as if all the bridges that spanned the spaces within me had been washed away. I was isolated on an island no one could reach. I lay unsure of what had happened, stripped of all surety.

I found myself whispering, "I've vowed myself to loneliness. For the rest of my life. Loneliness." Tears welled my eyes, pooling on the floor.

Someone called, "Anyone here?"

Footsteps came down the aisle between the two rows of beds.

I rose, brushing off my new habit.

"Sister Innocence," a voice said.

I had to peer at the nun standing before me because my vision felt blurred, not yet back in the present.

"Are you okay?" she asked.

I nodded.

"I was at the far end of the hall and heard someone scream. It was horrible. Like a trapped animal. I've checked all the dorms and lavatories and the other rooms. I couldn't find anyone. Did you hear it? It wasn't you, was it?"

"No."

She leaned over to pick up my evergreen crown. Handing it to me, she said, "You're pale. Your forehead band's crushed. Did you fall?"

"I tripped, but I'm okay now," I assured her. For several moments, she stared at me as if weighing the truth of what I'd said.

"You're sure?" she finally asked. Once again I assured her I was fine; she nodded in acceptance, turned, and walked out of the dormitory.

When I could hear her footsteps echoing down the hall, I sat, exhausted, on the straight-backed chair by the side of the bed. Finally, I rose, replaced my forehead band with a newly ironed one, finished packing, and left the fourth floor.

I was terrified. I'd just made final vows. I'd vowed to spend the remainder of my life at St. Cordelia's. *How was I going to do that?* I knew without a doubt that in making final vows, I'd said yes to living the remainder of my life in the loneliness now coursing through me. I did not feel equal to what lay ahead.

An almost paralyzing foreboding enveloped me. I felt as if I had fallen into a smothering abyss of despair. No longer did I feel God's presence. Nor did Arthur pad by my side. I was alone.

Part III

Profession

Innocent Laughter

That afternoon, Sister Mary Abram drove the St. Jude contingent of nuns back to our mission. The following day, I returned to the fifth-grade classroom. I never told anyone at the convent what I'd experienced in that dorm because I wasn't sure what had happened.

Way back in the sixth century, St. Augustine had recognized the lifelong presence of loneliness when he wrote, "You made us for yourself, O Lord, and our hearts are restless until they rest in you." Perhaps that was the answer: the restlessness of not being totally subsumed within God; the disquietude—and possible despair— that comes when we long for something that seems unattainable.

In the late winter of 1963, I had only one interpretation of that transcendent experience: I was to wear the cloak of loneliness the rest of my life. That assumption terrified me.

Yet there was still the life of prayer and the peace it brought. Still the feeling that I was connected to centuries of women who had prayed and lived this life. Still the nuns there on mission, each of whom was unique and who inspired me in different ways. Still those who made me laugh out loud when they told classroom stories with exaggerated gestures and raised eyebrows. Still the melody to which I danced in joy when I thought of being of service to God and to all human beings everywhere.

There was also still my own sense of humor, which remained in place during Holy Week—the week preceding Easter. Good Friday of that week commemorated the death of Jesus. In the convent, that day usually passed in solemn silence. However, in 1963 delight over a birthday gift broke that silence.

Two weeks before, Mom had sent me a book in care of Sister Mary Abram. After the superior gave it to me, I'd had no time to read until Good Friday, when the students were on vacation. That morning, I sat in my room, reading at my desk.

At the St. Jude mission convent, which had been built specifically as a dwelling for nuns and wasn't a refurbished Victorian home, each nun had her own private room with a bed, a desk, a chair, a sink, and a closet. We were seldom in our rooms during the day because of teaching and then praying, eating, and recreating together until bedtime.

On weekends, when we had time to sit in our rooms and read, we had to keep our doors open. On the morning of Good Friday, April 12, 1963, I sat in my room, door open, and began to read the book Mom had sent. Because she always made good book choices for me, I was eager to read the stories written by ten-year-old Virginia Carey Hudson in 1904.

As a child, Virginia had written a series of vignettes for a school assignment. The stories were about the adventures she'd had at home before attending boarding school that year. Fifty-six years later, in 1960, a relative discovered the stories in an attic trunk and published them in a slim volume entitled *O Ye Jigs and Juleps!* The tale I found hilarious on that Good Friday morning was about Virginia and her piano playing.

The girl's mother called her inside from play. When Virginia, barefoot, came inside, her mother asked her to play something for a very prim and proper matron who'd come to visit. The little girl thought she'd enliven the spirits of the straitlaced guest by performing a truly magnificent ending to her piano recital. When Virginia came to the last notes, she raised her right foot and struck the final key with her big toe.

I roared with laughter at this surprise ending and the image it invoked. Without thought for silence, I rushed out of my room. I simply had to share with someone the sheer exuberance of that little girl. In the hallway, several nuns, having been startled by my raucous laughter, stood glaring at me.

"Shhh!" I heard.

But farther along down the second-story corridor, I saw the face of Sister Sienna, the teacher with whom I often stood during recess on the playground. She was chuckling. On Easter, when I told her about the piano vignette, she, too, guffawed.

Ultimately, I left the book in the mission bookcase, hoping it would invoke laughter in all the other nuns who'd live there in the years to come.

Three or four weeks later I wasn't laughing as I sat in a surgeon's office with Sister Mary Abram. We'd come there several days after an appointment with a physician who, while examining my abdomen and pelvic area, had found what he called, "something suspicious." He'd set up this appointment with the surgeon who'd just finished his own examination and was now explaining the results.

"She has a large tumor in her uterus. It's sausage-sized and needs to come out immediately. I want Sister Innocence to check in the hospital tomorrow. I'll operate the next day."

He was addressing Sister Mary Abram, who took the place of Mother Morna Ann on mission. It was my body, but I'd vowed obedience. Sister Mary Abram listened, nodding her head in understanding.

Then, turning to me, she said, "You'll need to get lesson plans done tonight for a substitute teacher."

She then turned back toward the doctor, asking how long I'd need for recuperation before I could return to the classroom. He gave her some number of days; once again, she turned to me.

"For that many weeks," she said, "you'll need lesson plans. We'd best get back to the convent so you can get busy."

Slowly it dawned on me that I was to be operated on in two days. I knew nothing about what was going to happen or why this needed to be done. Without seeking the superior's permission to talk, I said to the doctor, "What exactly is a tumor and why does this one need to be removed so quickly?"

He began to explain what a tumor was and how it might be cancerous. That would be determined, he said, after he removed it. I needed the operation immediately, before the tumor had grown any larger. He explained that if it were cancerous it could spread to other parts of my body. That would mean the possibility of my dying.

All this was new information to me. No one in my family had ever had cancer. In fact, people just didn't talk about it. It was as if they were afraid that by mentioning it they might develop cancer. Because of this silence, I knew nothing about it.

I listened intently to his dire words, but something in me refused to accept them. I didn't think I had a tumor. I thought he was making mountains out of molehills.

Without turning to the superior and asking for permission to talk, I said, "I'm not having an operation on Wednesday. I'm teaching until school lets out. I'm not turning the students over to a substitute. We're right in the middle of an important project, and I'm going to be there to help them with it."

"You're taking a real risk," the surgeon said. "That tumor could grow. Metastasize if it hasn't already."

Sister Mary Abram remained silent. I appreciated her recognition that I was an adult woman who could make this decision. I knew, however, that because of my vow of obedience, I'd do whatever she decided was necessary.

Finally, she spoke, "Sister Innocence, you realize the risks?"

I nodded.

"And you have a real intuition, a belief, that there is no tumor?"

I nodded again.

"Then what do you think the doctor found when he examined you?"

"I don't know. Is there something besides a tumor that can form in the body?"

"A cyst," the doctor said. "They aren't as dangerous, but take my word for it, this isn't a cyst. It's a tumor. A very large one. Like bratwurst."

For a few moments, the three of us sat silent. Then I said, "I want to wait until school's ended. I'll come into the hospital the next day, but not before that."

I don't know why Sister Mary Abram let me get by with this blatant insistence on having my own way. She never explained. In fact, once we got back to the convent, she simply went into her office and I went to my room. We didn't speak of the operation again until school was over for the year. The surgeon had scheduled the surgery for two days after that.

The day after my initial appointment with the surgeon, I searched the school encyclopedia for a drawing of the uterus. I'd never had sex education in high school or college, so I was ignorant about that part of the body.

The illustration I found labeled the uterus, the ovaries, the fallopian tube, the cervix, and the vagina. All new words to me. Now I had something to picture. I also looked up the word *cancer* and went from there to hysterectomy, tumor, and cyst.

Between the day we met with the surgeon and the operation, I lay in bed each night picturing my uterus. I saw it as a large pink area pulsing with health. I saw each part in its place, nothing pushed aside by a tumor the size of a sausage. All was well. I had a healthy uterus. My body was perfect in every way. With that visualization and those affirmations in my mind, I eased into sleep each night.

The surgeon operated two days after school let out in late May. The next morning, he came into my room, sat on a chair beside my bed, and looked away, never once meeting my eyes.

"Well, Sister Innocence," he said, "when I operated I found only a cyst as big as the tip of my little finger."

With his upper body still turned aside, he held up his right hand, placed his thumb at the nail of his little finger, and demonstrated the size of the cyst.

"No tumor?"

"No. Just a cyst."

With those words, he rose and left the hospital room. I never saw him again.

When I left the hospital, Sister Sienna was there to drive me home to the convent. Because I had my college degree and had taken all the courses I needed for teacher certification, I was meant to go away to graduate school that summer. Recuperation from the operation put that off for a year.

My obedience that summer was to rest every afternoon for an hour and a half. One day, when I rose and left the dorm to go to Matins, I decided to take a short walk outside. As I drew near the entrance to the college chapel, a nun approached me.

"Sister Innocence, I'm surprised to see you out walking," she said.

"Why?" I asked, surprised in turn that my walking should seem unusual.

"Well, after a hysterectomy, you normally take a while before walking around."

"I didn't have a hysterectomy."

She frowned. "We were told to pray for you because that's what you were having."

I assured her I hadn't, but in truth I wasn't sure. Perhaps the doctor had done a hysterectomy and simply not told me about it.

A few days later Sister Mary Abram explained to me that the surgeon had planned on doing a hysterectomy. That's why the incision on my abdomen was nine inches long. On finding the benign cyst instead of the tumor, he'd simply removed it and my appendix and sewed me back up.

The scar healed into an inch-wide swath from my navel to my pubic area. At the time, no one thought professed nuns would ever leave the convent, much less wear bikinis. Given this, an unsightly scar meant nothing to the surgeon nor was it meant to mean anything to the nun. It certainly didn't matter to me; I'd never be married or want to have children. I thought no more about it.

There really wasn't time to think that summer about operations and their results because St. Cordelia Convent was celebrating its centennial. I was glad to be home for it and not away at graduate school. Sister Elise had composed an exuberant and joyous song about what we Benedictines were celebrating and what our lives meant. Daily we practiced. On the Feast of St. Benedict—July 11— we sang the song on the steps of the college chapel. It was a glorious time.

The lyrics Sister Elise wrote encapsulated the history of St. Cordelia's and the life of all of us who lived there. Two lines especially spoke to me: "Let there be laughter in the song we sing. Let it be measured to the lilt of prayer."

Despite difficulties with obedience and with accepting the other nuns as they were, I laughed a lot in the convent and out on mission. Not only at jokes, but also at the joy each of us got from the simple pleasures of the day. At recreation each evening, we'd share funny tidbits of the day's happenings and anecdotes that sent us all into gales of laughter. My name was Sister Innocence, but the convent itself produced innocence within each of us. That innocence, nourished by silence and prayer, often bubbled forth into laughter.

My Father's Gifts to Me

In late August I returned to St. Jude's. Most of the nuns who'd been there the year before also returned. Mother Morna Anne, however, had assigned a new mission to Sister Mary Abram, the former superior at St. Jude's. Now Sister Leona, a woman of very different temperament, served as superior. She was more excitable, her face betraying everything she was feeling. She'd raise her voice when upset and scold a nun in front of others. I'd now lived with four superiors, each unique, each individual.

That year I moved from a classroom of fifth-graders on the first floor to a second-floor classroom of sixth graders. As a group they displayed great curiosity about learning and the year promised to be a good one. That is, until Sister Leona called me from the classroom one morning.

The near death of my father marred that autumn. Mom called the mission convent to tell the superior that Dad had a ruptured aneurysm. The doctors had operated the night before and suctioned several pints of blood from his abdomen. (Or perhaps she said, "stomach." I'm not sure.) Mom asked Sister Leona if I could come to the hospital, which was only about twenty miles away.

A relative came to the convent, picked me up, and drove me to the hospital. For five nights, I slept at a local convent. During my time in the hospital, I was unaccompanied by a fellow nun, which was unusual because normally one nun always accompanied another, but the school could not spare two nuns from teaching.

I spent each of the five nights at the hospital watching over my father. As soon as Mom got there in the morning, someone drove me to the nearby convent of another order of nuns to have breakfast and to nap. When I woke, someone drove me back to the hospital.

Each night, I sat on a chair next to my Dad, who lay in a coma. I wiped him when he had a bowel movement and put a straw in his mouth when he seemed to want water. I held his hand and brushed back his hair, wet with sweat some nights.

As I sat by his bed, tending to his needs, the nurses encouraged me to talk to him. They assured me he'd hear. Following that suggestion, I began to tell him about life in the convent. About trying to be obedient and finding that hard. About the joy of prayer and singing. About the nuns with whom I'd lived and what I'd learned from them.

I sang him the songs he'd sung to me when I was a little girl.

I shared with him my memory of his cutting out paper dolls for me when I was three.

In the darkness of those hospital nights, I recited poems to him. I spoke to him of what these poems meant to me and why I'd memorized them.

I thanked him for all he'd taught me, especially the reading of newspapers. From him I'd learned to read the morning *Times* and the evening *Star* each day—a habit I sorely missed in the convent. I shared with him my memories of watching him open the newspaper when he got home from work and read it with great appreciation for news, letters, editorials, features. Even ads.

I also thanked him for his great patience in teaching me all sorts of things as I was growing up. With tears in my eyes, I told him I'd learned from him the patience that was part of my teaching style.

During those nights and days, tenderness welled up within me. I knew then that I truly loved my father despite how I felt about his drinking.

For a few hours each day Mom and I were together at the hospital and got to visit. Mostly we talked about what the doctors had told her.

"The doctors say that your father has a one out of ten chance of surviving," she said.

"One!" I was horrified. "Then he's going to die."

"No, Dolores," she responded, patting my hands. "That means he has nine chances to live."

"Mother, . . ." but she'd turned to talk with someone else in the waiting room. I turned to my right and repeated the conversation to my brother.

"She just can't accept what the doctor means," he explained. "In her mind he has a ninety percent chance of surviving."

When I heard the odds, I began to let go of my belief that all would be well. I visited with friends and family in the waiting room and tried to gently prepare my mother for Dad's death. She remained certain that all was well.

Mid-morning of the fifth day, the doctor came to the waiting room and led my mother, brother, and me down the hall to the door of Dad's room. Before we went in, he said to Mom, "I have some good news. The best. Your husband has made an amazing recovery. I gave him just one in ten chances of living and he's fine."

"I knew he would be."

"Be that as it may," the doctor said, his face bemused, "I think it was a miracle. I'm not big on miracles, but I think your daughter has powerful prayers. She brought about a miracle."

He turned to me as if I were the Holy Grail. I'm sure I blushed in confusion. I hadn't been praying in the waiting room, I'd been talking to cousins, aunts, uncles, friends and catching up on the five years since I'd left their world and entered the convent. I hadn't seen the majority of them for all those years.

I hadn't been praying the Divine Office or any personal prayers. I'd truly been remiss in doing anything connected to being a professed nun. It was my mother who'd been praying. She'd stormed heaven with her prayers. I had hoped that in the convent I'd become the valiant, faith-filled woman she was. That hadn't happened.

"Doctor," I said, "I haven't even been praying. If anyone has, it's been my mother. She's the one who prayed this miracle."

Once again he looked at me as if I were some beatific vision. "Don't be modest, Sister. I'm crediting you with the miracle."

I shook my head in denial. "No. Not me . . . "

Mom touched my black-sleeved arm. "Dolores, what does it matter? Your father is fine." She turned back to the doctor and thanked him for all he'd done, then asked when we could take Dad home.

I returned to St. Jude's that evening and resumed my teaching. A few weeks later, Mom wrote to tell me she'd gotten the bill for the hospital stay and the surgery for Dad. The doctors and surgeons involved had not charged her anything. When she'd called to ask about this, one of them said, "It was a miracle. Not our skill. We don't charge for miracles. You and your daughter are responsible for them."

I wanted to write those surgeons to tell them I'd had nothing to do with it, but I'd come to realize that people will believe what they will believe. I wasn't responsible for their thinking. I let go of my concern that once again I was living a lie. Clearly the surgeon hadn't seen behind the mask I wore.

On Friday, November 22, 1963, a little after 1:00 PM, Sister Leona announced over the school intercom that President Kennedy had been assassinated. The children and I gasped. Many of them cried, unsure what was happening. The news came in dribs and drabs. School closed early. That evening the nuns gathered in the formal sitting room of the convent. We huddled around the television that Sister Leona had rented that afternoon.

Again and again we watched the Dallas motorcade and listened to the ominous and definitive words of Walter Cronkite. Over the weekend, we witnessed the murder of Lee Harvey Oswald by Jack Ruby. We watched the swearing in of Lyndon Johnson as the 36th president of the United States.

On Sunday, a stunned audience of millions gazed at television sets and watched the horse-drawn caisson pass down Pennsylvania Avenue from the White House to the Capitol. Thousands of mourners entered the Capitol and passed by the bier of the dead president. On Monday we again gathered around the television and watched the funeral, intently listening to Robert Kennedy's eulogy. Finally, we saw the casket taken to Arlington Cemetery for burial.

That was the first time I'd viewed television since entering the convent in June 1958. During those dismal days, I wished that many more years could have passed without television if that would have meant that nothing so tragic as the president's assassination had taken place.

The year went on. Over Christmas, Sister Leona drove us up to the convent to spend a day with all the nuns who returned there during the holidays. This was always a special treat, especially for Sister Mary Cassie, who not only taught at St. Jude's, but did the nightly cooking.

Each Sunday she got a respite from the kitchen as each of us, in order, cooked the main meal. When my first Sunday came around, I felt stark terror. The only time I'd cooked at home, I'd set fire to the kitchen. The damage was extensive and Dad replaced the door, a window, and the stove. If I did that again—at the convent—what kind of penance would I get when I made culpa?

Sister Mary Cassie planned the Sunday menu; the assigned nun simply executed it. For my Sunday, she laid out two naked chickens to be baked. She also planned for me to mash potatoes with butter and steam some veggies. She'd spend the afternoon in her room across the hall—with the door open—while I prepared the meal.

The chickens were my undoing. When she handed their limp bodies to me, I asked, "Do I just stick them in the oven like this?"

"No, Silly! You cut them up into regular pieces. Thighs, breast, wings. Then you bread and bake them."

"I cut them?"

"Of course."

She handed me a slip of paper and said, "Here's the recipe for the breading mix. I've written down the baking time."

Handing me a knife, she departed.

I stood there, staring at those plucked chickens in all their nudeness. Bare-skinned and vulnerable. I grasped the sharp knife and set it against the skin that stretched between one chicken's lower body and one of it legs. Slowly I began to draw the blade across the skin. It was then I fainted, plummeting to the kitchen floor.

My body's impact with the linoleum brought Sister Mary Cassie racing back into the kitchen. She found me there, the knife having clattered across the floor and the chicken fallen from the counter and onto the skirt of my habit, which puddled the floor.

"What are you doing down there?" She said, shaking me to alertness.

"I'm not sure." She just stared, clearly waiting for a real explanation. "I've never cut a chicken before," I said.

She sighed, helped me up, picked up the chicken, and began to cut it and the other denuded creature into pieces, all the time muttering about some people who didn't have the sense they were born with. When she'd completed the task, she pointed to the breading recipe and the ingredients and said, "You'd best preheat the oven." Then once again she left the kitchen.

I dipped each chicken piece in a bowl of raw eggs and then into the breading. Then I placed the pieces on a cookie sheet and put it in the oven for baking. I set the timer and began to prepare the rest of the meal.

When the timer binged, I placed the chicken pieces on a large platter and carried it and the rest of the meal into the dining room. In that adjoining room, four tables set at ninety-degree angles to one another, creating a square with an empty center.

I rang the bell to assemble the other nuns for supper—twelve of us were there that year. We all sat down; Sister Leona led us in prayer and began to pass around the dishes. Everyone took a piece of chicken as well as mashed potatoes and gravy, green beans, cooked carrots, a slice of bread, and butter.

Sister Leona took a bite of the chicken and choked. Then I heard coughing from others around the table. All the nuns were gingerly placing their piece of chicken back on their plates. I took a bite and immediately realized why.

"This chicken isn't done, Sister Innocence," the superior said. "In fact, it's nearly raw."

I nodded.

"Collect each piece. Remember whom it belongs to. Then bake it again until it's done. Test it by tasting your own piece. No more raw chicken. Then ring the bell for supper. You understand?"

I nodded.

"No salutation for you tonight. You'll sit in chapel and consider the inconvenience you've put us through."

Supper was late that night. Afterward, the nuns recreated in the common room while I sat in the small convent chapel. One good thing happened as a result of my ineptitude: Sister Leona never again assigned me the obedience of cooking a Sunday dinner.

Conflicted

During recess that winter, a sixth-grade boy asked me what I thought of Che Guevara. Because we didn't read newspapers, watch television, or listen to the radio, I had no idea what he meant, but the term sounded like a place to me.

"I've never been there," I said. "I'm not even sure where it is."

"Sister, it's not a place. He's a man in Cuba. He's helping with the revolution."

"Oh."

It came home to me then, rather forcefully, that, except for the assassination of President Kennedy, I knew nothing of what had been going on in the world beyond the convent. Of great concern to me was my gross ignorance of what was happening in Washington, D.C. I no longer had informed opinions about the president's actions or the laws newly passed by Congress or the recent decisions of the Supreme Court.

I did have opinions about some of the teachings of the Church—teachings I'd been taught were infallible. In fact, some of my opinions represented unorthodox views of those teachings. That year at St. Jude's Grade School, one of my views came into question, resulting in clear disobedience on my part.

It all had to do with the loneliness of George—a student in Sister Sienna's sixth-grade classroom. He was heavier than his classmates and had a bad case of acne. I knew him because I taught reading to Sienna's students while she taught math to the students in my classroom. During the months of that school year, trust had been built between her students and myself. It was that trust that came into play in early April 1964.

One afternoon, Sister Leona, the school principal, called me to her office. She wanted me to talk to George about his touching his genitals in class. I was to tell him it was a mortal sin and that he'd go to hell if he didn't stop doing this.

I could feel my stomach clench. There was no backing away from a direct command by the superior. I was under obedience to talk to George and to say to him what she'd commanded. I knew, however, that I couldn't repeat her words because I didn't believe them.

I felt caught between two millstones.

That afternoon I asked Sister Sienna if she'd release George from class so he could help me carry a stack of English textbooks down to a first-floor storage room where we'd box them up. Having done that, George and I climbed the stairs back up to the second floor. When we came to the top step, I asked him to sit down with me as I was tired.

We chatted for a minute or two about the most recent short story he'd enjoyed in our reading class. Then I said, "What sports do you like, George? I've always liked baseball."

Grinning, he said, "Me too! I saw the Athletics play last night." He told me about his favorite player and what he'd done in the game. Then he said, "If I lost some weight, maybe I could be a baseball player. Do you think?"

"George, you just never know what's around the next corner for you. Set a goal and aim for it. Aim for the stars!"

He nodded his head several times. "I will, Sister. I will." He couldn't seem to stop grinning.

We had only so much time before the next class, and I needed to start talking to him about touching himself and masturbation. My hands felt clammy; I could feel sweat behind my forehead band. I had been ordered to talk to him and to report back to Sister Leona. I had to do that—I'd vowed obedience.

"George," I began, "I need to talk to you about something that I'd like you to change."

"What, Sister? I'd do almost anything for you."

I told him that I'd noticed he was touching himself in class. "Do you know you're doing it?" I asked.

"Yeah." He was silent a moment and then mumbled, his head bowed, "It's a habit."

"What makes you do it?" I smiled at him, trying to put him at ease.

"Kids make fun of me because I'm fat and I get nervous."

"It hurts doesn't it?"

"Yeah." He looked up at me. Tears pooled in his eyes. He whispered, "Sometimes I feel stupid when I answer in class."

"I'm sorry you feel that way. You're not stupid."

He looked down. I saw a whisper of a smile graze his face, then he muttered, so low that I had to lean forward to hear him, "It feels good, Sister."

When I said nothing, he looked up at me, his face streaked with tears. I nodded and said, "I know it does. It calms you down."

"Yes."

I waited a moment, then asked, "Does it make you feel less lonely?"

"Yeah." A slight smile lifted his lips as the tears continued to fall.

"It's okay to do it," I said. "It's just that some of the other kids and the grown-ups have noticed. It makes them uncomfortable."

"Why?" I could see he truly didn't understand. I took out my handkerchief and offered it to him. He took it and swiped his face. "Why?" he asked again.

"Touching yourself in your genital area is supposed to be done when you're alone. In your room at home. Or your bathroom. Or on your bed. It's no one's business but yours."

For a few seconds, he puzzled over this, still clutching the handkerchief, then said, "So I shouldn't touch myself down there when I'm in the classroom?"

"That's right. Just in private."

He thought about this, turning his head to look out the window in the stairwell. "Is it wrong?" he asked.

Now we'd come to what Sister Leona wanted me to say. I just couldn't. I could say only, "I'll be honest with you, George. A lot of people think it is. They call it masturbation."

He said the word aloud as if trying it on for size. Once again tears began to trickle down his face. Sighing deeply, he whispered, "Is it a sin?"

"Don't worry about that."

He began to fold the handkerchief into smaller and smaller squares. Finally, he looked at me, his face sadder than usual. "But you're telling me I can at least do it at home, Sister? It makes me feel good. Not like I'm a nobody."

"Just do it in private. By yourself."

We both took a deep breath. "Okay," he said. "Okay."

He handed me the folded handkerchief as we walked to the boys' restroom. I encouraged him to splash cold water on his face to erase the tear streaks. When he came back out, I walked him to his classroom.

Before he opened the door I said, "George, you're a brave young man."

He looked at me, surprised I thought, then grinned and entered the room.

Later that day, Sister Leona asked if I'd spoken to George as she'd requested and told him that he was committing a grievous sin.

"I did speak to him. He won't be doing it in the classroom anymore." She was satisfied; so was I.

The idea of masturbation being a mortal sin that could send someone to hell simply didn't seem right to me. God had given us bodies with sexual urges. As long as doing something sexual didn't hurt anyone else, I couldn't see the harm. Nor did I believe that the Church had a right to tell us what God thought.

I didn't express that view to Sister Leona. Back in 1957 during my senior year of college I'd learned to keep my mouth shut about my private beliefs. Back then I'd ceased to believe in angels. When the chaplain found out, he had threatened to expel me from school. From that I'd learned to keep my maverick opinions to myself.

I couldn't tell that lost sixth-grader what I didn't believe. Still, all this was an indication that I wasn't keeping my vow of obedience. I still considered my own opinions and my own beliefs to be the most enlightened ones. Once again, I found myself at odds with the life I'd chosen.

That summer, I went away to graduate school to begin a master's degree in Benedictine Spirituality. During the eighteen months I spent in the novitiate I had never left the convent grounds: the cemetery, the two chapels, the main convent building, the novitiate, the laundry.

On the three missions to which I'd been sent, my world had consisted only of the school buildings, the parish church, and the convent. I'd never gone shopping nor been in the home of one of the students. My life was restricted to a few buildings and the playground. Only when Dad had been in the hospital had I seen just a little more of the world.

The summer of 1964, I boarded a train with four other nuns and traveled to another Benedictine convent and university. There I took a class on the Desert Fathers of the third and fourth centuries CE, another on the Psalms, and a third on the Rule of St. Benedict.

One of the nuns who traveled there with me that summer was someone toward whom I felt antipathy because of her relationship with Sister Michael. Even in college I had wanted her to like me better than anyone else. She'd now found a more mature friend than I—Sister François.

During the two scholasticate summers Michael and I shared, I wanted to spend the evening recreation—between the ending of supper and the beginning of Compline—with her. I wanted her to pay attention to me. Once again, as I had when doing the laundry obedience in the novitiate, I began to act fey. To put on a show of innocence and mysticism. Of mystery. There's no doubt I made a nuisance of myself.

She grew weary of my infatuation and let me know that she wanted to have little to do with me. Perhaps she wondered if I were a lesbian who was sexually interested in her. I don't know. I'd never felt sexual stirrings for anyone, what I did feel was a great need to be important to someone. A great need to be the center of someone's existence.

I'd felt this deep-seated need since kindergarten. I felt jealous when friends paid too much attention to other people. The truth was that I bought into the ancient belief that there is only so much worldly wealth and so much love. If either the wealth or the love was given to someone else, it wasn't there for me. I had no idea that love freely given can expand and embrace all humankind.

In the summer of 1964, when I traveled to graduate school with Sister François, I felt a deep and abiding jealousy, deeply resenting her "taking away" my friend. During our first days at graduate school, she invited me several times to stroll around the campus. Wanting nothing to do with her, I refused. She persisted.

More days passed and her dry wit, which left other nuns laughing, began to intrigue me. The next time she suggested we walk, I accepted.

She was, I quickly discovered, both funny and interesting. By the end of the summer, when we returned to the motherhouse, I fully appreciated why Sister Michael cared about François. Crestfallen, I also accepted that I couldn't "compete." Grieving the loss of Michael's friendship, I began to avoid her when we met. I truly was an "all or nothing" person, too immature to balance a relationship in which I always wanted to be the center of attention.

While all this was going on that summer, I had a strange experience. The nun in charge of the study program explained that in order to get a master's degree I needed to pass a proficiency test in a foreign language. I'd had three semesters of French in college, but ten years had passed without my reading anything in French.

Still, the program director wanted me to take the test that first summer. If I failed, I'd have two or three more summers to pass. She explained that for the test I could select any theological book written in French. I'd have the summer to translate and study it. Then at the end of summer school, she'd choose a passage from the book and I'd translate it.

One of my favorite writers was the French theologian Jean-Guenolé-Marie Daniélou, a Jesuit. I found his writing lyrical and had read one book that appealed greatly to me. It was this book I asked to use as the one from which the passage for my translation would be selected. The program director consented.

I spent much of the summer reading that book in both English and French. Because of its beauty of expression, one particular chapter enthralled me, so I spent the most time on it. When the Saturday came for me to translate a French passage, I discovered that the program director had selected that chapter. The angels, whom I professed not to believe in, had surely watched over me.

The Second Vatican Council of the Roman Catholic Church convened in October 1962 when Pope John XXIII called the bishops of the world to Rome to explore the relations between the Church and the modern world. The Council, which closed in December 1965, brought great change to convents around the world. In truth, the Council cracked open what had been set in stone for centuries in religious orders.

At St. Cordelia's the changes—the fractures in the structure of religious life—began as early as 1964 when the nuns began to pray the Divine Office in English. Changes in long-established customs such as kneeling to ask permission from a superior followed. For me, the greatest change was that we could read select books and magazines that would keep us in touch with what was happening in the world. After the assassination of President Kennedy, we were also given permission to watch television news on a daily basis as well as other programs that might help us teach more effectively.

Mother Mary Maude, who'd been elected prioress in 1962, encouraged all of us to become knowledgeable about what was happening in the world around us. She believed that only by becoming enlightened could we best serve others.

Unfortunately, not all superiors on mission followed her example. At the next mission, where I spent two years, we had no magazines or newspapers and no conversation about what was happening in our world. At other missions, however, the superiors did enact many of the changes Mother Mary Maude suggested. Those missions became a little more lenient because the superiors welcomed change.

In truth, although I took advantage of the changes, they came too late for me. When I let myself, I could feel the roots of anger inching downward, deep into the dark recesses of my heart—anger at my parents, the convent, and myself. Ruthlessly I suppressed this growing rage. Despair followed. No longer was there a song of praise in my heart.

Stuttering Begins

After summer school I returned by train to the motherhouse. Within a few days, I'd received my obedience for the next nine months—teaching high school in another farming community. The next day, seven of us piled into a car for the trip to St. Martin of Tours parish. We would help staff its grade and high school. Sister Mary Saul was our superior. It was the first time she'd been assigned that position.

The convent building itself was a converted two-story Victorian house. The attractive front door opened into a wide foyer and to the staircase that led up to the second floor. The spacious first floor contained several rooms, among them the kitchen, pantry, dining room, and parlor. On the second floor was a storeroom, a lavatory, a large room for recreation, the superior's office/bedroom, and three bedrooms in which the rest of us slept in twin beds—two to each room.

Because I'd never taught high school before, I initially had to spend a great deal of time studying the books I'd be using. The high school was small, probably only about one hundred and twenty students. I was to teach the English classes. That meant studying literature, grammar, and the fundamentals of writing. I also was to direct the school plays, oversee a school newspaper, and shoot and develop the photographs for it.

I'd had many fine teachers in grade and high school as well as college, so I had a wealth of memories to call on about how they'd taught. The teaching at St. Martin's was enjoyable because the students wanted to learn.

Also enjoyable was watching a dramatic series on television from 7:30 to 8:30. Entitled *Mr. Novak,* it was about a first-year English teacher in Los Angeles. Sister Mary Saul gave permission to watch because she thought the program might give us some teaching ideas.

After a few episodes the other nuns decided they'd prefer to recreate upstairs in the common room. I was eager to watch. Each Tuesday evening found me in front of the television, enjoying the drama and realizing that Mr. Novak got much more personally involved with his students' lives than I ever had. I didn't know whether that was a good or a bad thing, I knew only that the routine of a nun's life wouldn't permit such involvement.

As a new superior, Sister Mary Saul insisted on following convent and mission rules to the letter. Up to 1964, the nuns had used flannel pads for their monthly menstrual periods. In the novitiate we'd each been given a large piece of flannel out of which we made two-dozen squares, which we hemmed on the sewing machine. We also sewed a nametag to each pad.

After using a pad, we'd wash it in the laundry room, squeeze out the excess water, and rub a bar of soap over the stain. Then we'd roll up the pad and put it in a bucket so that the soap could seep into the stain and help remove or dim it. On Saturday, we'd put those pads in the laundry for washing. Then they'd be ready for use the next month.

I'd done this for six years, but in September 1964, Mother Mary Maude, enacting a welcomed change, sent each mission a gross of sanitary pads—144 boxes with twenty-four pads in each box. Of the seven nuns who were there that year, only three of us were still menstruating. Clearly, we had many more boxes than we needed.

When my period began that September, I knocked at Sister Mary Saul's door, knelt by her desk, and said, "My period has begun. May I have some sanitary pads?"

"Yes. Go to the storage room and take one."

I thanked her, removed a box of pads from the storage room shelf, and put it in a drawer in my bedroom. Three days later, Sister Mary Saul called me into her office.

"Sister Innocence," she said, "did you not get your period?"

"Yes. The pads are wonderful. Thank you."

"You say 'pads.' The question is what are you doing for pads? You must need more than one."

"There are twenty-four in a box."

"I didn't tell you to take a box. You were to take one at a time."

"You mean I need to come into your office each time I need a pad?"

"Exactly."

Even then, when I was trying so hard to be perfect myself, her dictum seemed ridiculous. However, I followed her instructions for the two years we lived together. After that the mother superior assigned me to the Academy, located in the administration building next to the convent. There I asked for and received a whole box of pads.

That experience with the sanitary pads at St. Martin of Tours was one example of Sister Mary Saul's adherence to the letter of the law. Another involved my going with the students to speech meets in several cities throughout the state.

On the morning of the first Saturday meet, she summoned me to her office. "Sister Innocence," she said, holding out a small change purse. "Here's the money you'll need for lunch." I thanked her and placed the purse in my pocket.

"Do you have everything else you need?" she asked.

"Yes. I have all the speeches and the program." I mentioned other things I was taking along just in case the students forgot the order of presentations and the times.

"Do you have a handkerchief?"

Surprised by such attention to detail, I nodded.

"Let me see it."

I pulled it out of my pocket and showed her. Every time I accompanied the students to a meet we went through the same scenario. Always we ended with me pulling out my handkerchief. Again and again, I had to remind myself that I'd taken a vow of obedience.

A third example of my having difficulty with obedience at St. Martin's has to do with an auditory disability with which I was born. From kindergarten through third grade, I missed three out of the nine months of each school year because of asthma. That meant that I never learned to sound out words. I knew the names of the alphabet letters, but I didn't know that each letter had its own sound. Nor had I ever learned that words had syllables and each syllable had a vowel within it.

In grade school we had spelling books. Each week we learned how to spell twenty new words. Each night—Monday through Thursday—I would memorize five of those words. Mom would point to one, for example, *winter*, and say aloud the word those letters represented.

I didn't know that the letter beginning the word represented the sound of *w*. For me, the word *winter* could be spelled *egtyrhgwt*. It wasn't a series of melded sounds; it was an arrangement of randomly chosen letters someone in the far distant past had put together.

I didn't recognize the sound of individual letters or syllables. Mom had said, "winter" and pointed to the letters. For me, they became the configuration that was pronounced "winter." It never occurred to me that in that word are two syllables *win-* and *-ter*. Or that *win* is the sound of a *w* and an *i* and an *n* melded together.

I memorized the configuration of the letters *w-i-n-t-e-r*. Whenever I saw this entity in a sentence or on a Wheaties box or in a headline, I knew I was seeing the word *winter*.

Throughout grade school, I memorized all the words this way. They were not a combination of melded sounds of alphabet letters. They were simply an arrangement of letters that someone—I didn't know who—had decided would be said a certain way. Later I realized that this was the same way that Chinese ideograms have to be learned.

All was well as long as the teacher based the Friday test on the twenty words in the speller. My memory was good and I could remember the shape of the connected letters when she said it. For the word *winter*, my mind came up with its shape, arrangement, configuration, and structure. It was like a landscape covered with snow except for a tall tree in the middle. That, of course, was the letter *t*.

All this worked well for me for eight years. Then came high school. For the first three years we didn't study spelling as a separate subject in the curriculum. In my senior year, however, Sister Marlene taught us English literature. Each day she assigned our class a reading from the textbook. The next day she'd begin the period with a quiz of ten words she'd chosen from the selection we'd read.

We never knew what those words would be. Sometimes the text was so erudite that I simply couldn't memorize all the words that might appear on her list. I couldn't divide unfamiliar words into syllables and sound them out, much less pronounce them. I simply saw a word I didn't know and mostly figured out its meaning in context. Thus, when Sister Marlene said a word, it was cloaked. That is, I often had no idea as to what letter started the word, much less what letters followed.

Sister Marlene paced up and down the aisles, announcing each of the ten words. For each word she said, I scribbled a group of letters on my lined paper. She completed her list, then continued striding as she spelled the words correctly for us. We determined our score and gave it to her to record in her grading book.

Sometimes, all the words eluded me: 0 out of 10. Sometimes, I conquered as many as 3. For me, that was cause for celebration. Sister Marlene, however, thought I could do much better.

Each day, she doggedly called my name: "Dolores. What today?"

I gave her my score. Immediately, she rounded the aisle and strode to where I sat. Muttering all the while, she rolled her sheaf of papers into a cylinder and bopped me on the head with it.

Sometimes exasperation overtook her, and she continued to bop my shoulders and upper arms. I ducked, but her aim was good and it was only paper. In our class of twenty-six, I ended up being the valedictorian. Thus, it's not surprising that she suspected I was being contrary each day by doing so poorly on the spelling quiz.

"Stop fooling around, Dolores! What was your real grade?"

"I got one right."

"You're mocking me! Tomorrow I expect 100 percent from you!"

Ha! That never happened.

Years later, my inability to sound out and spell words became a stumbling block for me at St. Martin of Tours.

Here's what happened: Whether at the convent or on mission, the superior waited for the bowls of food to be passed and a paragraph or two from a spiritual book to be read before giving salutation and permitting us to talk at the table.

I was the youngest nun at St. Martin of Tours, so Sister Mary Saul gave me the obedience of reading the passage each evening. The book she'd selected had many personal names that I'd never before met as well as innumerable four-syllable words. I had a good reading vocabulary but frequently didn't know how to pronounce words I'd read. Looking up the word in a dictionary didn't help because I couldn't interpret the pronunciation squiggles.

Each evening, the nuns passed around the dishes of food and left them all in an arc before my plate at the end of the table. I'd read for about three minutes—or however long the passage for the day took—and then stop. While reading, I'd stumble over words that I didn't know how to pronounce. I'd make up something but was never sure.

On my first mission, Sister Emma had helped me with pronunciations. There I'd learned that each alphabet letter had its own sound or sounds. Because of that realization, I'd gotten much better at sounding out words, but I still stumbled over long words and proper nouns.

When I completed the reading, I'd sit down and Sister Mary Saul would grill me over the mispronounced words. She'd spell a word from the reading and ask me how to pronounce it. I would be unable to respond, so she'd pronounce the word then listen as I said it aloud five times per her instructions. Next, she'd ask me to spell it and say it again. We'd do that for every word I'd stumbled over and mispronounced that evening.

The result of this daily grilling was twofold: the other nuns' food got cold while they waited for me to get the words right, and I began to stutter when I read aloud at the evening meal and when I spoke to Sister Mary Saul at any time. I became so conscious of my mispronunciations that I feared using any new word with her just as I feared that I'd been mispronouncing words all along. I stuttered for months and stopped talking during our meals and at recreation.

That is, I responded with minimal words to a question, and I never began to speak unless spoken to. The only place my speech remained normal was in the classroom. The students accepted the way I spoke. For the remainder of the school year, I continued to stutter when I spoke to the superior or the other nuns. It was only when I went home to the motherhouse that I gradually was able to return to normal speaking.

Longing for Home

By mid-winter of my first year at St. Martin's, the superior must have connected my stuttering with the reading I did at supper. From that time on, Sister Verity, who was a few years older than I and taught grade school, did the obedience each evening. Verity had entered the convent right after graduating from high school, so she'd probably been teaching at mission schools for close to fifteen years. As that first year passed, I realized that Verity was a compendium of all the rules devised by the superiors whom she'd met at missions where she'd taught.

On one of those missions, a superior must have said that no street crossing was ever to be done on the diagonal from opposite corners. I suspect this because the first time we left the house to go to the post office, we walked to the corner of our street. I stepped off the curb and began to walk diagonally across the street. She turned to the left and walked the edge of a square to the opposite corner. Arriving there, she walked to the corner where I stood, waiting for her. In my mind, we could save steps walking on the diagonal. The town was small. Few cars ever passed by, so crossing that way was safe. Why not do it? As she came to where I stood, she began to reprimand me for not following the rules.

"No one ever said to me that we can't cross on the diagonal," I countered.

"Well, Sister Edythe told me on the last mission I was on we couldn't. . . . You never follow the rules. Who do you think you are?"

All the way to the post office on Main Street, she muttered about my lack of obedience. My recalcitrance. My not even being able to read. Which meant that she had to do it when everyone knew that it was a job for the youngest person on mission.

This harangue occurred every time we left the convent to get mail. I began to find not only the situation, but also the nun, strange. Unlike myself, she was obedient in every way. Something must be wrong with me to find her so odd.

I was now twenty-eight, just ten or eleven years older than the seniors I taught. The two other high-school nuns—Sister Mary Saul, the convent superior and school principal, and Sister Yolanda—were older. In fact, Sister Yolanda was a little senile.

Several times during that first year, I overheard the students making fun of her, mimicking her. One Saturday when we'd driven home to the motherhouse for a visit, I went into Mother Mary Maude's office to tell her what was happening.

"It's not right," I said. "In fact it seems downright wrong that a nun who taught well for so many years should have to end her teaching career with mockery."

"Sister Innocence, we have only so many nuns to fill all the positions in the schools where we teach."

"I know, but . . ."

"Nuns have to teach past retirement age if we are to fill those positions. I'm sure Sister Yolanda does no harm."

"That's not the point," I said. "The students ridicule her. That's not fair. All these years she's done her best. She's been a success. She shouldn't have to end her career with failure."

Mother Mary Maude dismissed me with a thank you for the information and a reminder that she had to do the best she could for everyone—for the students, the nuns, and the parishes.

I returned to St. Martin of Tours parish determined to talk individually to the students Sister Yolanda taught. I hoped to call forth from them their kindness and understanding. Many of them stopped their teasing and began to carry her books from one classroom to another. They shushed other classmates who persisted in taunting her.

As the month passed, some of them continued to torment her, but more often than not their fellow students rejected this behavior and soon incidents of it became rare. I felt such relief because their initial actions had seemed so cruel to me. Now Sister Yolanda was finally given the respect due her age.

The death of my grandmother—my mother's mother—shadowed the spring of 1965. She had lived for over forty years in the Ozarks, where she'd farmed two hundred acres. A few years before her death, she sold the farm to a young couple and began living in a rather ramshackle three-room house, papered with pages from the Montgomery Ward catalog. It had an outhouse and a well and was near her dear friend Hattie. Both of them lived on a country road that was about two miles from town and a half-mile from a country general store.

When I'd visited her as a child, Grandma told me a story about Hattie that always made me laugh even while I felt sympathy for her grandson whom the story featured. Grandma's story went like this: "Hattie says to her six-year-old grandson, 'Zeke, go to the store and get me some chewin' tobackey and some cornmeal.' She hands him some change, then turns away. As he starts for the door, she calls him back and says, 'And Zeke, if there's any money left over—' His heart lifts. Maybe. Just maybe she'll let him get an ice-cream cone to eat on the trek home. His hopes are dashed when she says, '—get me some more tobackey.'"

That story and many others that Grandma told me about the farm and its history were part of my memory. I treasured them and felt great gratitude when Mother Mary Maude permitted me to attend the funeral. Once again, the convent allowed me to go somewhere without an accompanying nun. This represented the changing of customs that came about because of Vatican II.

The day of the funeral two things happened that stayed with me when I returned to my mission home: one reinforced my view of myself as an actress performing the role of a nun; the other intensified my desire to be in my true home again—with my parents.

On the way to the cemetery, I sat in the back seat of a limousine with my mother's older sister. As we traveled the rutted road, she talked about my cousin, who'd entered a teaching order in Oregon at age sixteen in 1952—six years before I entered St. Cordelia's.

"I've seen her since she entered," my aunt said. "She knows how to conduct herself."

"How is she?" I asked. I hadn't seen my cousin since she'd entered. At one time we'd been real buddies.

"Oh, she's fine. She's a model nun. Unlike you."

I stared at her. What was she trying to say? But I didn't ask; instead, I thought to myself that my aunt had recognized just how unsure of myself I was. Just what a forgery I was. She'd recognized this after being with me only one day. Surely everyone at the convent recognized the same thing. I wasn't a saint. I was a sham. A fraud. An imitation of a real nun.

I enjoyed a good visit with my brother at my grandmother's funeral. His life was busy with family and work, so I'd seen him only once or twice since entering. As children, we'd squabbled but had often been mischievous together. Now, many years later, an opportunity came for us to walk together after the family meal following the funeral; I was overjoyed. Filling me in on what was happening in his life, my brother talked about his wife and children, his work, and bass fishing. I talked to him about teaching and about the life of a nun.

Two or three times during that walk I searched for an analogy to illustrate what I was saying. My brain had never been good at originating analogies. I could see them when others used one, but I couldn't see relationships clearly enough to form an analogy. Each time I searched, my brother would come up with one. That was a sure sign to me of his broad and deep intelligence. I knew then and there that he not only had much more common sense than I had but that his mind was sharper, more perceptive.

I found myself missing his sense of humor and remembering what had happened on one of my visits home from college in the fall of 1956. When I walked into the living room, he'd picked me up, swung me over his shoulders in a fireman's lift, and begun to sing, "You Ain't Nothin' but a Hound Dog!"

I'd screamed and then laughed out loud until tears rolled down my face. Amused, Mom and Dad watched the two of us from the open doorway. Those moments in our front room had stayed with me as one of the happiest of my childhood. Dad wasn't drunk, and we were all laughing . . . together.

Walking with my brother on that dirt road with dust puffing up and around our shoes, listening to his tall tales, seeing his roguish grin and the Irish gleam in his eyes, I felt the deepest longing for family I'd experienced since entering the convent. My brother, who

I'm sure had no idea that I'd ever thought about leaving St. Cordelia's, brought home to me the memory of when I'd been simply a young girl. Giggling often. Wearing twin sweater sets. Rock-and-rolling. A young girl whose favorite spot in a world of possibility was the creek meandering through the farm where she grew up.

I longed for home.

Mom Intervenes

In June 1965, following my first year at St. Martin of Tours, I decided that leaving the convent was my only option. I felt myself rebelling again and again at being obedient; I didn't want to do what others told me was best for me. Quite simply, the deep streak of independence, which my parents had always encouraged, refused to be quelled. My love for the Divine Office couldn't counter that.

The day after returning to the motherhouse for summer vacation, I knocked on Mother Mary Maude's office door, entered, knelt, and asked permission to leave the convent. Innate kindness and compassion suffused her countenance as she sat, her coifed head inclined, listening intently, as I poured out all my muddled thinking. My great weariness. My longing for a life in which I could relax from the quest for perfection.

Gently, she reminded me that the convent did not demand perfection, that I was my own taskmaster. I didn't disagree with her. I knew I had imposed on myself the dictate of being perfect. I had let my need become an obsession.

Her eyes filled with compassion, Mother Mary Maude told me she understood and respected my decision. She asked only two things of me: would I participate in the yearly retreat and would I talk over this decision with my mother. Mother Mary Maude said she'd invite my mother to come for a visit after the retreat ended.

During the next week, I listened to the retreat master as he explored the precepts and charism of St. Benedict. Praying for guidance, I sought a pathway out of the chaos of my own mind. Two days after the retreat ended, with me still uncertain about reneging on my vows, Mom drove up to St. Cordelia's. We met in the recreation room of the college administration building. While in college, I'd tasted in that room the joy of being away from my father's drinking and of making lifelong friends. Joy eluded me now; the past seven years tasted like Lenten ashes.

"What's happening with you, Dolores?" Mom asked once we'd sat down at one of the oak tables in the recreation room. The straight-backed chairs were hard, just as were all the ones on which I'd sat for seven years.

"I just can't stay here. It's too hard. It doesn't feel right anymore."

She looked at me, her eyes deep pools of love. Then she talked about how she'd stayed married to Dad despite his drinking. "Dolores," she said, her palms cupping my coifed face, "when you put your hand to the plow, you never look back."

"It's stifling me, Mom. I can't breathe."

She looked at me, as if memorizing my face, enclosed in the white linen coif, the starched headband, and the black veil of profession. Softly so that I had to lean forward to hear, she said, "When we set our hand to the plow we look ahead. We go down one row and then another. Each is different."

"The furrows here all look the same, Mom. I want to stop. Go back to the barn."

"Dolores, you've never been a quitter. You've taken vows. I imagine they're pretty demanding. That doesn't matter. You take them; you live them. Just as I have. You don't look back. You look ahead."

"All I see ahead is sameness for the rest of my life."

"Then that is what your life will be." She stroked my cheek with her right hand and sighed. "Dolores, just because things get hard we don't walk away from them. We stay. We make them better."

"Has your life gotten better, Mom, because you stayed with Dad all these years? Is he still drinking? Has he raped you recently? Or tried to kill you?"

My words seemed to stun her. Tears trickled down her pale cheeks. I rose so quickly that the chair on which I'd sat toppled over. "Mom, I'm sorry. I'm so sorry. I shouldn't have said that." I held her close against my chest. Her tears fell on my white coif, softening its pleats.

"Dolores," she whispered. "My life isn't yours. You have security here. It's what you wanted back when you entered. You've set your hand to the plow. Move forward. No one's life is a bowl of cherries."

"Mom, life has to be more than this for me."

"Stay for another year and see if it doesn't get better. Look ahead beyond the end of the furrow. There's a future for you here."

She looked up, her eyes imploring me to reconsider.

I stayed.

After Mom left that day, I walked slowly down the college hall, past the music rooms and the college chapel, and into the convent proper—the motherhouse. A little distance down the linoleum-clad hall was the entrance to the office of the prioress. Mother Mary Maude welcomed me and my decision. Like my own mother, she hoped that another year of prayerful reflection might calm the tempest within me.

Before leaving her office that day, I learned that earlier that year she'd registered me for summer school at Marquette, a Jesuit university in Milwaukee. I appreciated her not telling me about this when I'd asked to leave. Knowing how much I loved to learn, she could have used schooling as an inducement to stay. She hadn't. She'd deferred to my decision to leave. I'd always admired her. Knew her to be a woman of deep spirituality. Now I felt genuine love for her.

The summer before, I'd studied Benedictine Spirituality. Now she wanted me to begin work on a master's degree in English. The following day I boarded the train to Milwaukee where I spent the next two months taking classes in Old English and studying the literature of that period.

The convent asked three things of those of us who went away to study: to pray the Office; to celebrate the Eucharist daily; and to study and do well in our classes, which were expensive. This wasn't a hardship for me. I'd always liked to learn new things and both prayer and the Mass were blessings in my life. The Eucharist was, in fact, a time of thanksgiving; I had a lot for which to be grateful. I was getting to study another language—Old English—what could be better than that?

Every weekday after class, I entered the coolness of the campus church. Gesu was spacious, like a medieval cathedral. On July 2, 1965, I went there to celebrate the feast day of Mary's visit to

Elizabeth. A Jesuit priest, one I've never before heard preach, stepped up to the lectern.

"Today's Gospel relates an exciting event!" he announced. All of us gathered at Gesu gazed at him expectantly.

Beaming, he said, "Just think of it! Mary comes to visit Elizabeth. One's really old. One's young. Only a teenager. Both are pregnant. They're big with child. Big. Think of it. . . . Big." He spread his arms wide, his hands rounded as if holding an enormous ball.

My funny bone began to vibrate.

He continued. "What happened when Mary says 'Hi!' to Elizabeth? . . . I ask you. What happened?"

I waited with baited breath.

"I'll tell you what! That baby in Elizabeth's womb gives her one swift kick and laughs out loud. Right there in her womb—kickin' and laughin'."

I laughed too, bent over with my face pressed against my thighs—laughing so hard I began to hiccup.

"One swift kick! Elizabeth knows something's going on. Then Mary tells her about Jesus. John kicks again. Another swift kick. Those women are sittin' there gossipin'. Sippin' tea. And John's just laughin' and kickin'. For joy! Pure joy! Can you see it?"

I could.

I walked out of Gesu that afternoon singing Gershwin's "Summertime." My body swayed to the words, "One of these mornings, you're going to rise up singing, then you'll spread your wings and you'll take to the sky."

I spread my black-clad arms wide, lifting them toward the sky. I danced back to the building where we nuns lived for those three months. That day and throughout the rest of summer school I felt equal to anything, whether it be reading Old English or composing modern poetic sentences based on the alliteration found in *Beowulf*.

It was there in Milwaukee that I met women from other religious communities. In 1958—the year I entered—Catholic women had a plethora of orders from which to choose: Dominicans, the Nuns of the Sacred Heart, Little Sisters of the Poor, CSJs, the Carmelites, Benedictines, Maryknoll. The list seemed endless.

The nuns I met in the summer of 1965, were from these orders and several others. They served God in many different ways, depending on the charisma of their founder. That founder had chosen some specific work by which to bring the message of the Gospels to the world.

So young women in high school or college or in a workplace asked themselves, "Do I want to teach? To nurse? To nurture? To fight for justice? To help the poor? To do missionary work? To care for orphans?" Given their response to this question, each woman chose an order.

Each evening in the community room or our residence hall, we told stories about the founders of our order. As I listened with great curiosity, the other nuns, one by one, described their work among the poor or in hospitals or in other countries, such as China and El Salvador. They described their daily lives and the rule that governed their religious lives.

I learned that the vows all of us had taken differed a little from order to order as did the traditions, rules, regulations, routines, schedules, and prayer life. This surprised me because I knew so little about convents. As I listened to how their lives differed from that of Benedictines, I realized that I had entered a convent that was stricter than many others. However, while all of us had entered different orders, we were One in our desire to serve God by serving others.

As the days passed, I realized that although the classes I was taking were important for a master's degree, the camaraderie of all these nuns was the greatest gift of that summer. Despite our different work, we all wanted to share God's bountiful love with others through our service.

One of the things we talked about during those evenings in the large residence hall, where all the nuns stayed during the summer, was our vocations: how we'd come to enter a convent. This, too, was immensely interesting to me because many of the nuns had entered the order that taught them. That was only partly true for me.

The Sisters of Mercy, founded in 1831 by Mother Mary McAuley, educated me in grade and high school. In 1842, a small group of indomitable nuns had come to the United States from Dublin, Ireland, to set up Catholic schools and to work with poor women and children. The nuns who taught me for eleven years were excellent teachers, but I was never inspired to enter their order. Teaching held no appeal for me.

Nor did the Benedictine professors at the St. Cordelia's College initially inspire me to enter the convent. The inspiration came only after my transcendent experience in the math classroom on April 10, 1957. As I walked later on the campus, I realized how at home I felt with the Benedictines. I felt they represented centuries of learning. More importantly they prayed the Divine Office. The next day, desiring to pray, I asked the college dean how I might enter the convent.

That summer of 1965, while studying at Marquette, those of us who were nuns not only recreated each evening, but each morning we walked several blocks to the buildings where we'd take classes. The nun who was taking the same classes as I often walked with me. Sister Eugenia's habit was different from mine. Not only was it a different color—blue, it also featured a different forehead band and head covering.

Eugenia had the ability to imitate how each professor in our classes spoke and taught. I'd beg her to imitate the professor who taught us Old English. Several times that summer, she made me laugh so hard I dropped my textbooks on the sidewalk and stumbled over them. The two of us had to hold our bellies as they shook with laughter.

Those summer months were two of the happiest I'd spent in the convent.

During that same summer, St. Cordelia Convent established a daughter house in a state across the country. A number of nuns transferred their vows to this new motherhouse. Transferring vows was necessary because one taken by Benedictines was stability, which meant that a nun vowed to spend her life at the convent of her vows. Most of the nuns who transferred their vows to that priory had taught at some point in the schools of that faraway state and loved the people there—especially the Hispanic population.

Among those who decided to transfer their vows were my two dearest friends—Sister Michael and Sister Yvette. Both had taught in that state before, but each year, at the end of their nine months of teaching, they'd come home to the motherhouse. That had given me the opportunity to visit with them; laugh with them.

Now, they would no longer walk the convent halls in the summer or sit at the refectory table or do obediences. I might never see them again. I felt bereft.

That fall I returned to St. Martin of Tours. The staff in the grade school was the same. In the high school Sister Mary Mildred had taken the place of Sister Yolanda, who'd retired from teaching and was now staying home at the convent. I was relieved that Mother Mary Maude had made that decision—to keep Sister Yolanda at the motherhouse. Mother couldn't do that during the 1964-65 school year because she had no one to take Yolanda's place, but by the fall of 1965 one of the scholastics was ready to go out to teach.

Most of the time, only nuns taught in Catholic schools. However, lay teachers sometimes taught a course when no nuns were available. During that second year, a male lay teacher— Daniel—taught social studies and history. He and I became friends. Often, after the school day ended, we'd talk about what was happening politically beyond the farming community in which we taught.

Daniel educated me in the history of our involvement in the events taking place in South Vietnam, which I still knew as French Indochina. He explained that in May 1961 President Kennedy had sent four hundred Special Forces personnel to that Asian country to train South Vietnamese soldiers and that in 1964 Congress had passed the Gulf of Tonkin Resolution. In February 1965, the United States had sent its first combat troops to South Vietnam. Daniel filled me in on what had happened in the intervening months.

Throughout the remainder of the school year, he kept me up to date about what was taking place in that war-torn Asian country and in Washington, D.C. He clarified for me the "domino theory" and why fear of its consequences motivated President Johnson and Secretary of Defense Robert McNamara.

A Quaker and thus a pacifist, Daniel was against US involvement in Vietnam. Patiently he detailed his stance and how it differed from the way President Johnson, Robert McNamara, and General Westmorcland viewed the situation. He brought in newspaper articles for me to read and news magazines like *Time* and *Newsweek*.

Sister Mary Saul, my mission superior, allowed me to watch one television program each week. However, she had not subscribed to any news magazines or newspapers, nor did she encourage any of us to look at the news on television. I was thirsty for news of the world beyond the convent, so I deliberately disobeyed her and avidly read everything Daniel gave me.

I knew that in confession, the parish priest would tell me to stop reading. Rationalizing that I wasn't hurting anyone, I didn't confess. If I were going to stay, I needed more freedom. Mother Mary Maude and the convent council were slowly enacting changes that would provide that freedom, but these modifications weren't happening quickly enough for me.

My actions indicated how attached I was to my own will. Inwardly, I was saying, "I know best. I'll choose the time for change." With little remorse, I read the articles and newsmagazines Daniel gave me. Then I hid them on a shelf in the high school maintenance closet.

Daniel wanted me to actively engage in peaceful protest against US involvement in Vietnam, but I wasn't ready for that yet. At the time, that would have meant leaving the convent, and just a few short months before, I'd made the decision to stay. He did help me sort my thoughts and accept that the government could and did lie to us. Because of him, I became more realistic about politics and, perhaps, about life.

He also helped me with the yearly presentation of three senior-class plays. I directed the plays; he did the lighting and helped the students paint the scenery. That meant we spent quite a bit of time together, but nothing either romantic or sexual developed between us.

What did happen excited me more than that: He challenged me to think. I don't know what he found in me to like, but he found something—maybe a willing student of politics. If Sister Mary Saul suspected anything, she never asked me about it. I was grateful for her trust even as I realized just how duplicitous I was being.

At some point during my two years at St. Martin of Tours, the state legislature began to debate abortion—this was several years before the Roe vs. Wade ruling of 1973. One school day Sister Mary Saul called me into her high-school office, handed me a postcard, and explained that the legislature was considering the legalization of abortion in cases involving incest or rape. She wanted me to write to our state representative as an anti-abortionist. I refused to do so.

"You think abortion is moral?" she asked.

"I haven't thought about it. I don't even know much about abortion. I need to study the question and see where I stand."

"You'll stand with the Church is where you'll stand."

"Where's that?"

"The Church believes that all life is sacred and that life begins at the moment of conception in a woman's womb."

"I'll still need to study this."

"Sign the card."

So, once again, as I'd done in November 1960, I refused to be told what to do politically. No one was going to tell me how to think. The sorry truth is that I'd never even heard the word *abortion* before, and I wasn't even sure of what it meant. I knew only that I wasn't going to be told what to do politically. My parents hadn't raised a civic conformist.

This rebellion didn't represent serious thought or discussion; it simply indicated my innate stubbornness. Later I realized that my uninformed decisions were simply that—uninformed. If I were to become politically active, I needed to read. Study. Research. Listen to views from every side.

Perhaps, if we'd been allowed to speak of the past in the convent, I would have returned home to St. Cordelia Convent each summer and explored ideas with my friends there. We would have differing views, and I could have listened to their thoughts on perfection and living the Rule. I could have broadened my own narrow view of saintliness. I could, perhaps, have become a more mature woman. That didn't happen.

My Own Worst Enemy

That second year at St. Martin of Tours, I became aware that money from the federal government was readily available to buy supplementary material for teaching in public schools. Because the state had hired the nuns to teach at the grade and high school in the small farm community, both schools were public. We didn't teach religion in them, only secular subjects.

With a generous budget for visual and audio aids, I searched catalogues for slides and films to enhance the material I was teaching in the literature classes. I taught all four years—freshman through senior—and purchased sets of novels for each class.

For the seniors I selected *The Lord of the Flies* by William Golding. The students, especially the boys, responded to it with great enthusiasm. Dennis, a young farmer whose grades were poor and who seldom completed his homework, said to me when we were midway through the book, "If you'd get more books like this, Sister Innocence, I'd read 'em all!"

He was the same student who recognized a speech pattern I used when I was upset. One day I was talking to the students about their use of "Hell!" in the classroom when they wanted to express their disgust.

Raising his hand, Dennis said, "You know, Sister, when you say 'fiddle-dee-dee' and 'fiddle-dee-foe' that's your way of saying 'hell'."

The other seniors held their breath, awaiting my response. Relief lit their faces when I broke out laughing and said, "You're right!" Recognizing that what the seniors said and what I said had become habits for us, we worked together that year to lessen our use of "hell," "damn," and "fiddle-dee-dee."

Another of my obediences that second year was to monitor the young adult choir each Sunday at Mass. I'd sit at the top of the choir bleachers with my back against the wall, watching for any hijinks or visiting between the students. The problem was that I often found things to laugh about. Knowing my weakness, the students would sometimes make an effort to tickle my funny bone. I'd hastily hide my face behind a handkerchief and relapse into giggles.

The students didn't have to make any effort on Christmas morning 1965 when the parish priest gave his homily. I expected a sermon about the joy of Christmas or the life of simplicity seen in the crèche or the kind of intangible gifts we could give one another.

Instead the priest stepped before the pulpit, tapped the microphone, and said, "Christmas—a rat race!"

I shook with laughter, picturing rats scurrying up and down the towering Christmas tree in Rockefeller Center. They cracked one bauble after another, climbing upward, waving at the television viewers. I'd seen that New York tree on television during the 1950s; the beauty of it had awed me.

Several students, seeing my reaction to the sermon, laughed with me. Their stirring alerted Sister Mary Saul, the choir director, that something was amiss. When she turned and saw me—handkerchief pressed to face, shoulders shaking with mirth—she, too, broke into a grin. The priest went blithely on, sermonizing about how our consumerism made a rat race of Christmas. None of us in the choir loft listened. We chortled instead.

Each evening in the convent we had an hour's worth of recreation when we knitted, crocheted, and visited, telling stories about the day's happenings in the classrooms and any news we'd heard about the community and the farmers. I often played chess with Sister Mary Mildred who was in her seventies.

For several consecutive nights, we played the game until Sister Mary Saul told us we were being too exclusive and needed to recreate with the other nuns. Mildred muttered, "What's the world coming to that at my age she's talking about a particular friendship!"

During that second year at St. Martin of Tours, I finally admitted that seeking perfection was devastating me. I continued to think about the past instead of living in the present. I thought about all I longed for: my parents, lying on a couch talking over the day with them, going barefoot, raiding the refrigerator, having the freedom to do what I wanted to do when I wanted to do it. Always I was aware that by living in the past, I was rebelling against my vows of obedience and stability.

More and more I became aware that a routine that left no time for solitary leisure didn't satisfy me. It had in the novitiate. There the novelty of making no choices about what to do and when to do it had left me stress free for eighteen months.

Now I remembered the wide creek flowing through the farm on which I'd been raised. During the warm days of spring, summer, and fall I'd spent at least part of each day sitting by myself on the banks of that creek. The sound of water rippling over the rock-strewn streambed soothed me, took me to a dream state that opened up vistas for me. I missed that; I missed dawdling.

Having to be someplace at a certain time each day, all day, was too rigorous for me. I felt the center of myself crumbling. I wanted to read novels and meet characters whose lives were far different from mine. I wanted to know what was happening in the world. I wanted to discuss politics. To talk about the past.

I wanted.

I wanted.

And that was the problem. I wanted what I didn't have in the convent.

I also began to feel sexual urges. Not toward Daniel or the parish priest or any other man or woman, but just the need to be held, to be close to someone. Ever since a neighbor had molested me in grade school, I'd feared intimacy.

Because of that I'd seldom dated in high school or college and had always been reluctant to even kiss a boy. The foreign stirrings of desire I now felt alarmed me. I began to understand why the sixth grader at St. Jude's had masturbated. For me to do so was to break my commitment to chastity. I felt as if a dark abyss of doubt was dragging me ever downward.

In the spring of 1966, a farmer and his wife approached Sister Mary Saul after Mass one Sunday. They asked if she and the other nuns would visit them in the new home they'd built. They invited us to tour the house and have a picnic with them.

Two problems presented themselves with this invitation: Nuns did not eat with "lay people" except for the ceremonies of getting the habit, making first vows, and making final vows. Also, nuns seldom went into the homes, even of their families, once they'd made vows. Even if a family member was sick and the nun went home to see that person, most of the time she'd stay at a local convent and not in her former home. In this instance, Sister Mary Saul decided we could visit the new home. However, we wouldn't eat with the family or go inside the house.

The following Sunday, the seven of us piled into the car for our trip out into the countryside to the new farmhouse. On a table set up in the side yard, the couple served us a lovely meal. Then they left the yard and went inside.

They must have been watching from a side window, however, because as the last of us finished our dessert, the couple came back outside. Inviting us into their new home, they beamed with pride. Their excitement was contagious.

I'd never felt that the missions in which I'd taught each year were homes. The furniture wasn't comfortable. No comfy couches or armchairs. No prints on the walls by Degas. Turner. El Greco. No lights by the single beds for reading far into the night. Nothing that wasn't austere—to my eyes. I'd never particularly thought of this, but as I approached that house in the spring of 1966, those thoughts engulfed me.

As we approached the front steps, Sister Mary Saul said to the couple, "You know, we're not allowed to enter your house, but I thought we could go around it and look through the windows."

Her words poleaxed me. Here were this man and woman, delighted with their new home and eager to share their joy with the nuns who were teaching their two young children. Spurning obedience, I said, "Sister Mary Saul, we can't refuse to go inside. They've invited us here. Fed us. Why are we being so rude?"

Shushing me, she motioned to the other nuns to follow her to the first window. They gathered around it, their black habits edging up above their ankles as they stretched to peer through the windows. With their hands shading their eyes, they seemed like a flock of curious crows. I stood at a distance, not wanting to be part of the carnival.

Then, glancing at the couple and their two children, I realized they felt I was the one being rude and ungracious. Quickly, I joined the other nuns and followed them from window to window, always standing in the back, but leaning forward slightly as if to see inside the house. I felt we were following the letter but not the spirit of the Holy Rule . . . and surely not the spirit of the Gospels.

Before the sun set, we returned to our mission convent. Sister Mary Saul called me into her office where I knelt as she remonstrated with me for being obstreperous. I listened, feeling shame that I'd offended the couple with my rebellion and regretting the day I'd decided to stay in the convent.

When I entered the convent, I'd hoped that through prayer I'd develop a rich inner life. The convent wanted that to happen for each of us who embraced the religious life. Instead of growing more grateful for the joy of following Christ Jesus, however, I had become introspective, obsessed with my flaws. I began to concentrate on myself rather than on the community in which I had hoped to serve God.

In many ways, I became scrupulous. I thought that not only was I not suited to the convent because I couldn't live the vow of obedience but that I was a charlatan living with people who thought I could. In other words, I began to think too much. To dwell on myself. To become self-centered and self-absorbed. A general malaise settled about me. My usual enthusiasm for teaching waned.

One Saturday I was in the kitchen wiping the dishes when Sister Mary Saul said, "Sister Innocence." I turned and saw her standing on the landing.

"Yes?"

"You're not well. You need to see a doctor."

I insisted I was healthy and needed no doctor's appointment.

"You're ill. We need to find out what's wrong."

"I'm not."

She sighed deeply. "You're gaunt. Listless. You're going to see the doctor. Repeatedly you've been disobedient. I'm tired of living your vows."

With great clarity I realized that her vision of life in a convent and mine differed. Hers was probably the correct one, but I held fast to my own need to exercise independence.

"You don't live the vows for me," I said, "Your job is to create the conditions under which *I* can live my vows."

My words seemed to stun her. She asked me to repeat them; I did. Then she turned and went back up the steps to the second floor. A few days later she told me to get ready to see the doctor. She'd made an appointment for me. The next week she drove us to the doctor's office. He examined me and found nothing untoward except that I was too thin. He prescribed more rest.

My thought afterward was that Sister Mary Saul was trying to be a good superior. She'd been concerned about me, and I had thrown her concern back in her face. Nevertheless, I was unable to let go of a subliminal anger, which was so submerged I didn't even recognize it as anger, only as unease.

Why did I have to ask permission to use each individual pad during my period? Why did I have to display my handkerchief like a child each time I accompanied the students to a speech meet? Why was I told during recreation that I had to sit by this person or that one? And why when I read for the meals my first year there had I been corrected on my pronunciations so deliberately?

Rebellion grew in me. It was perhaps the rebellion of a teenager, not an adult. Had I been emotionally mature, I would have gone to Mother Mary Maude and told her what bothered me. With great understanding and wisdom, she would have helped me work through this. I didn't do that. Instead I got moody. Withdrawn. Imbalanced.

Equilibrium fled.

I thought that if I talked to another nun I'd be failing in charity. I wouldn't be living in the present. Daily I fought a battle within myself. When I thought negative thoughts about Sister Mary Saul, I castigated myself. I blamed myself for my stubbornness and my failure to appreciate the goodness in her. All this was my fault. Slowly my disappointment in myself devoured me.

Entering the Labyrinth

In June of 1966, twelve months after my first requesting to leave the convent, I once again entered the Prioress' office, knelt, and asked to leave. My second request startled Mother Mary Maude even more than the first. After all, only a handful of professed nuns had left the convent in its previous one hundred years. Given that, my persistence was historically atypical. Once again she asked me to make the convent retreat and to spend time considering my decision.

The retreat was a particularly powerful one. It brought me back to why I'd entered in the first place: to my love of the liturgy and the Divine Office and my wanting to dedicate my life to something—Someone—larger than myself. I got caught up again in the beauty that was the convent life. In the Rule of St. Benedict. Caught up in admiration for all the women who were dedicating their lives to prayer, to service, and through their actions, to the manifestation of God's love for all. The simple truth was that at heart I loved the *idea* of monasticism.

When the June retreat ended, I went into Mother Mary Maude's office and once again knelt by where she sat. In my usual sophomoric way, I declaimed, "I'm staying, and if I ever again ask to leave, remind me of this. I'm committed to staying." That had always been my way. To make sweeping announcements as if my words were the axis on which the earth spun.

Within a day or two, I traveled to the university, where I'd spent the summer of 1964 in pursuit of a graduate degree in Benedictine Spirituality. When I returned home later that summer, I received my obedience: I'd be teaching in the academy attached to the motherhouse for the coming year.

A day or two before the other nuns went out on mission, I was walking down the first-floor hall of the administration building, intent on some errand. At the building's entrance a group of nuns, all a few years older than I, stood chatting. Among them was Sister Mary Henry, a woman of great tenacity with a sense of the ridiculous. When I'd lived on mission with her three years before, we'd become friends. Her way of looking at life had helped me keep things in perspective.

Now I overheard her say, "Here comes Sister Innocence. Let's ask her. She always has something beautiful to say."

My heart clutched. Was that the reputation I had? That I said beautiful things? If only they knew what ugly thoughts jousted one another within my mind. How judgmental I was.

Sister Mary Henry asked my opinion about something. Whatever I said at the time was innocuous, yet they all smiled as if I'd pleased them. Thinking of myself as a performing, wind-up doll, I left them and continued down the hall. The façade I wore fooled them. Only I knew just how brittle it was.

Decades before, the Benedictines had established Cordelia Academy for girls in a few rooms. It now occupied two floors of a large building. The faculty taught classes on the third floor; the boarders lived in dorms on the fourth. These dorms ranged in size from as many as forty beds to as few as fifteen.

Each dorm—freshmen, sophomore, junior, and senior—had a prefect who sat in the hall each morning and evening and on weekends to be available to the girls. The prefect served as a surrogate mother, laughing with them, commiserating with them, talking with them about their forays into dating.

Besides teaching that year I served as the prefect for the sophomores. They slept in St. Philomena dorm. She was one of the four Roman Catholic patrons of lost causes. Rather quickly this obedience became a lost cause for me. When I first began, all went well; the sophomores and I enjoyed one another. While teaching six and a half years before, I'd learned that my role was to be someone students could trust, someone from whom they could learn. As a prefect I needed to provide security for these fifteen-year-old girls who were away from home for nine months.

Each evening I sat in the hallway across from the entrance to St. Philomena. A number of sophomores settled themselves on the floor around me and shared the happenings of the day: What they thought of the food in the cafeteria. Which boy had flirted with which girl at the dance the previous Friday night or the football game. Together we laughed over their foibles, rejoiced at their successes, and grieved their failures.

All that changed toward the end of September when Sister Cory, the prefect for the seniors, began to find fault with me. Throughout the next three months, she'd troop down the hall after the sophomores departed for their first class and ask me to observe the dorm through her eyes.

She'd see the beds made without tucked-in corners; the towels that didn't hang straight; the drawer that wasn't closed; the chair that wasn't flush to the bed; the worn slippers lying on the floor and not in the hall locker. Each morning she'd recite the litany of things I wasn't catching and demand that I be harder on the students. She scolded me as if I were a recalcitrant teenager. "You have to whip those sophomores into shape," she insisted. "Like an army drill sergeant."

Her demands seemed unreasonable to me. Rigid. But I was an amateur at prefecting whereas she was a veteran, having taught in the academy several years. Thus, I accepted her dictums as the Bible for prefecting. My sense of humor deserted me in my quest to be perfect as a prefect; I became unnecessarily tough on the sophomores.

Their response? Most avoided me. Others made snide remarks. Still others began to devise ways to torment me.

The more incompetent I felt as a prefect, the more effort I put into teaching. In mid-June Sister Mary Maude, due to illness, had stepped down as prioress, and we elected Mother Mary Sybil to succeed her. Assigning my obedience in August, the new prioress explained that she wanted me to devise a new religion program for the academy students. This religion program should reflect the decisions made during the Second Vatican Council. When asked why he convened the council, Pope John XXIII had replied, "I want to throw open the windows of the Church so that we can see out and the people can see in."

Mother Mary Sybil wanted me to incorporate the theology I'd studied at summer school as well as all I'd read from the leading theologians of the day. Many of them had influenced the decisions that flowed out of Vatican II with regard to doctrine and dogma. It was clear that she was continuing the work Mother Mary Maude had begun of bringing the convent into the modern age.

In response to her mandate, I came up with the idea of a weekly master lecture to each class: freshman, Monday; sophomores, Tuesday; and so on. Weekly, each student received an eight-page booklet from an educational publisher. That "reader" provided the topic on which I expanded in our master classes. Each Friday the students met in smaller groups with a member of the staff who responded to questions and built on the lecture I'd presented earlier in the week. I provided handouts for the staff.

Both the students and the staff responded whole-heartedly even as I found myself thinking more deeply about what I truly believed with regard to Roman Catholic doctrine and dogma. I entered a dark night of doubt. Upon examination, so much of what the Church taught made little sense to me, but I was teaching in a Catholic school. I had to teach what the Church taught.

At the time, many theologians—such as Hans Kung, Bernard Haring, and Edward Schillebeeckx—were pulling apart the pat answers I'd been taught throughout my years of Catholic education. They tried to find the bedrock for Catholic dogma and doctrine, the meaning of which had been lost or disguised in the nearly two millennia since Jesus walked the earth and Paul catechized pagans around the Mediterranean basin. These theologians were, quite frankly, returning to the message of the Gospel, those faith documents of the first century.

In these classes I attempted to help students become critical thinkers who would search the kernels of truth in their own experiences. I didn't do this so that they would reject the teachings of the Church—I certainly hadn't done that—but I did want them—and myself—to be Roman Catholics who understood what being wholly human meant and how the Church helped them become all they were called to be. We all had such great potential to become fully human, as Jesus had been. Throughout the United States other teachers were also exploring this humanistic approach.

Besides teaching religion, I taught two senior classes of English Literature. While in graduate school I'd become enthralled with the etymology of words. I shared this newfound knowledge with the seniors by providing them with Latin and Greek roots, suffixes, and prefixes used to form many English words. Using those roots, we made up new words and delighted in our creativity.

That fall we studied *Macbeth*. During the first day or two, I acted out several scenes for the students, taking all the parts and emoting as if I were treading the boards of the Globe with Shakespeare himself. As the seniors lost their shyness over performing, I invited them to act out the scenes—sometimes one student playing several roles and sometimes a role per student.

We fell to the floor in death, stabbed and rubbed out the stain of blood, ranted and raved, parried and thrust. We had a grand and glorious time. In that English classroom I felt buoyant. Beyond that room, a glacier of desolation encased my emotions, yet with those seniors I felt both secure and creative. Assured.

By late September, the seniors so enjoyed our English literature class that they began to amble down the long fourth-floor hallway each evening. They settled on the floor by where I sat at the wide entrance to St. Philomena's dorm. Their visits seemed to increase Sister Cory's combative and dismissive attitude toward me. Whenever I left the security of the third-floor classrooms and climbed the stairs to the minefield of the fourth-floor I felt conflicted. The urge to flee hounded me.

These nightly visits from the seniors annoyed those few sophomores who still wanted to talk with me in the evening. They complained that the upperclassmen were infringing on their turf. I did nothing about this. In my classes each day I used up all the energy I had. Nothing was left in reserve for prefecting. By the time the classes ended, I wanted to collapse from exhaustion.

I descended deeper into an abyss of duality. In the classroom I felt a clarity of vision that prompted me to forget myself. Each day I performed brilliantly. I was doing the best teaching I'd done since I'd made first vows, yet I was failing miserably as a prefect.

Any surety I had, even about talking with the seniors, eroded as Sister Cory began, in her morning forays to the sophomore dorm, to mock the way I taught religion. She belittled the humanistic method; she chided me for being a clown in the English classroom and not displaying proper decorum.

Slowly I lost any ability I had to keep convent life in perspective. I had become a stone statue, unable to move beyond my own despair. The song of praise I'd felt on entering had deserted me. No longer was I able to dance to the music of the Universe. I stood still.

One night in early November I heard voices in the foyer to my bedroom. At first, I thought a few sophomores were making mischief out of their dislike of me. Wanting to tell them to go back to bed, I got up from my own bed and went into the foyer. This narrow room, with its built-in drawers that contained toiletries, connected my bedroom to the main hall. Switching on the lights, I saw no one. Thinking that the sophomores must have heard me get up and then scurried to their dorm, I turned back toward my bedroom door. Suddenly, someone spoke.

"You're such a numbskull," the voice shouted with disdain.

I turned toward the far-left corner, ready to tell whoever had snuck back into the foyer to keep her voice down. I was afraid she'd wake all the sophomores asleep in the adjoining dorm. But the voice had not come from a student. Standing in that corner was a woman in her thirties, wearing a tweed business suit with a jeweled brooch pinned on one lapel. Her rounded body seemed real enough, and yet through it, I could see the woodwork around the door. I gasped. Confused.

Then another voice spoke.

"We mean you no harm, Sister Innocence. In fact, I, for one, would like to help you."

When I turned toward the far-right corner, I saw a woman dressed in a lavender pullover and a pleated skirt. She looked to be in her mid-twenties. Tentatively, I stepped toward her, wanting to touch her arm, wanting to know if I'd touch flesh or if my hand would go through her and touch the wall cabinets.

Another voice.

"I don't like the dark. Monsters might get us. Let's go back to bed." The voice came from behind me. Turning once again, I saw a young child, no more than five or six. She held out her hand toward me and said, "Please, come back to bed. Shoo away the monsters."

Slowly, I backed toward the bedroom door. In three of the corners of the foyer stood three presences. They were present and yet not like any humans I'd ever met before. They had to be imaginary. I needed to get back to bed. To close my eyes and let go of this dream. To sleep and wake the next day. They'd be gone then. Surely they'd be gone. Wouldn't they?

I backed toward the bed; they followed, the child settling next to me, the two women sitting down, one on the straight-backed chair and one on the windowsill.

"I need to sleep," I said to them.

Each answered. The first woman said, "Who's stopping you?" The second, "Yes, you get up early each day. You need your sleep." And the child whispered to me, "Please pull the covers over me." I did. Sleep came and the night passed.

When the hall bell rang the next morning to awaken the students and prefects, the three presence were still with me in my bedroom. They watched me dress in my habit, commenting, about my weight loss. As they walked with me to my classroom, they told me their names: Anna, Dolores, and Dodo.

The three became my constant companions. Anna, I came to realize, was a dictator; Dolores, a peacemaker; Dodo, a child who'd always been loved. Throughout my waking hours, they accompanied me everywhere, talking to me and to one another.

I had enough sanity left to realize that I was living in two worlds: one—that of students and faculty and nuns—was real. The other—the one inhabited by those three presences that others clearly did not see or hear—had to be a projection of my imagination. Daily the power of that alternate universe spread its tentacles into my teaching. Whenever I spoke to someone in the world that I clung to as real, the fully clothed presences, standing in the corners of whatever room I was in, listened and commented.

"What a dumb thing to say," Anna sniggered. She had an insistent voice so strident I had a hard time hearing what any student was saying in the classroom.

Dodo, a cheerful child, responded, "I liked it."

Dolores turned to Anna and commanded that she leave me alone. "She's doing her best," Dolores insisted.

Momentarily they distracted me from teaching as I looked at them in the three corners and saw the expressions on their faces: Anna frowned; Dolores looked concerned; Dodo grinned. Each dressed in clothes I'd worn throughout my life—a sundress and sandals on Dodo; faded jeans, T-shirt, and sneakers on Dolores; a subdued gabardine suit, silky blouse, and high heels on Anna.

Daily they tormented me with opinions. My head ached from trying to figure out who was saying what. Had I just heard the voice of a presence or a student?

Trying to listen to the students above the din within exhausted me. Anna, dressed in her usual business suit, never stopped censuring me. I always measured up short for her. In her pinafore, Dodo couldn't recognize a mature thought or emotion if it had turned cartwheels for her. Dolores, attractive in her two-piece sweater set and slim skirt, tried to arbitrate, but Anna's know-it-all voice riveted her too.

I was careful not to show I heard voices and saw invisible multiple forms of myself. I'd observed the behavior of others for years and knew what was perceived as normal. I produced it now. I acted.

That acting depleted me. I lost weight. Since grade school I'd been 5 foot 4 inches and had weighed 118 pounds with little fluctuation. Now I was down to 103. My face, encircled by the coif, became gaunt. Quaking under the expectations I thought others had of me, I moved farther and farther away from allowing myself to feel.

Sleeping became problematic. Fearful of the specters, I began to get up and go into the room where the students watched television each evening. The programs so engrossed me that the voices stilled for a while. Night after night, I'd watch television for hours, then return to my bed.

When I wasn't watching television into the early hours, I was lying in bed thinking of all the novels I'd read during my years of schooling. I examined the plots of the classics I'd met in college. I revisited the scenes of the historicals I'd checked from the library in high school. I reintroduced myself to all the characters I'd ever met in the countless novels I'd enjoyed.

I longed to have a thick book of fiction to read. In it I would be able to live for hours in another world. A world far from the convent and the sneering presence of Sister Cory. *If only my life were a novel,* I thought. *I could live there and never emerge from the pages.*

But then again maybe I already was. Maybe I was living with Alice and the Mad Hatter. Maybe I was only a character in a novel that would end and I'd sleep within the plot. Safe.

Days passed; I spent each night watching television or living within a novel I'd read before entering the convent. Little rest; less sleep. Morning came. I mumbled my clothing prayers as I donned habit and scapular, coif and veil. With these I girded myself for the next act. Each day I walked the halls, bone weary, unable to frame words until entering the classroom. Then I'd turn an inner key and perform.

I knew I had entered the labyrinth of a nervous breakdown, but I was such a gifted actress that no one seemed to realize just how emotionally bruised and mentally ill I was. In the midst of this confusion, my one certainty was that I'd failed in everything I set out to be as a nun.

My big concern was that others—students and nuns—would soon realize just how far down the path of madness I'd already traveled. I knew I couldn't keep up the act indefinitely. I was sure that if I stayed I'd end up in the state's mental institution. A nun on my first mission had told me that when someone from the convent "lost it," she spent the rest of her life in that facility. Other nuns were there. Soon I—and the three presences who accompanied me—might be also.

The three of them seemed grafted to me, accompanying me everywhere, even to the place that had always been a haven—the choir chapel. It was there that Anna began to snidely insist, "You don't have long to live."

Darkness Descends

By Thanksgiving week I fell apart. In classrooms I expended all the physical, as well as psychic, energy I had. Beyond those windowed rooms, I felt depleted. When students spoke to me in the hallways, I managed to smile and act interested. Yet, moment by moment, I turned on and off the switch of personality. I acted normal, then retreated to apathy.

Everyone treated me the same as always. They seemed to sense no difference, yet I walked slower and slower into the day. Words eluded me. Holes riddled my brain.

Despite this, I continued to smile. One student even said, "I love your smile, Sister Innocence. It's like you know some secret. It's peaceful." In reality, I held myself together with the glue of will. Warfare raged within.

During the two years I'd spent on my previous mission, I inwardly sobbed my persistent loneliness and frustration. I felt anger, then upbraided myself for judging others as well as the very life I had chosen to live. Emotional tides swept me from the shores of certainty to the depths of disorientation.

What happened now, when I was stationed at home in the convent, teaching in the academy, was the shudder of an existential earthquake. My belief in God's love had eroded, leaving nothing but shreds of memory. I didn't think he believed in me anymore. We were lost to one another.

After a day's teaching, I'd enter the choir chapel, trying in its peacefulness to retrieve myself and the God I'd lost. I found nothing there—nothing but the three presences. The words I chanted with the nuns tasted like death in my mouth. Everything was gone. All surety. All belief. All hope. Everything crumbled around me. I walked warily down the hall fearful that the floor would suddenly quake, a deep fissure would open beneath me, and I'd plunge into the beckoning abyss.

Some time that fall I went down to the first-floor office of Sister Ellie. However, she, too, was experiencing difficulties. A few months before, she'd confided that she was going through menopause and realized she'd never be able to have a child. The realization hit her hard. That may explain why when a young nun from another convent enrolled at the college, she became so important to Ellie that my former mentor had time for no one else.

This was perhaps an example of a too-close friendship. Not a lesbian friendship, but one so immediate that it closed the two of them off to others. Perhaps it was infatuation, as I'd felt for Sister Michael. Several times in late October and early November, I knocked on Ellie's office door. She'd invite me to enter. I'd open the door a crack and find her seated with the younger nun. Ellie would say, "Sister Innocence, I'm busy right now. Would you come back another time?" But another time never came for she was always with someone.

Because Sister Ellie wasn't available, I went down the hall to Sister Claude's office. She'd taught me philosophy in college. Her intellect and down-to-earth appraisal of life had always somewhat intimidated me because my idealism and romanticism seemed immature next to her realism. Now I was desperate and knocked at her door.

Two or three times that fall I tried to talk to her about how I felt, but I couldn't let myself really tell the story. Always I thought I'd be revealing my failure and my lack of perfection. With my stilted words I'd be judging others. I couldn't let myself complain because saints didn't complain. They simply had the wisdom to take whatever unpalatable medicine life handed out and swallow it. I was a wimp and couldn't do that.

Even as I tried to seek Sister's Claude's counsel, I suppressed my feelings, just as I'd always done. I veered between judging the convent harshly and feeling guilty about doing so. My anger bruised all my judgments.

By late November of 1966, I felt only my ineptitude. Whatever was wrong was my own problem. Something must be reprehensible within me for life to become so dark. All the other nuns were content. Why wasn't I?

To my surprise, right after the last sophomore left on Thanksgiving week, Sister Claude came to my room next to St. Philomena's dorm. "Sister Innocence," she said, "I have a room ready for you in the college residence."

"But . . ."

"No buts. You need rest. I'll bring you your meals. You'll just sleep."

Like a zombie, I gathered my toiletries. We walked together over to the residence hall. For the next five days I slept, waking only to use the bathroom and to eat whatever food Sister Claude brought me. Only on Sunday afternoon when the boarders returned to the academy did I get out of bed and dress. Late on that November afternoon, Sister Claude walked with me back to the main building. I thanked her, assuring her I felt rested. What I didn't say was that I felt as if dead seeds rattled in the cavity of the dried gourd I'd become.

Monday found me back in the classroom, teaching religion and English Lit. Even though I'd slept continuously over the Thanksgiving holidays, I felt no peace. I was simply a wind-up doll. Now, before stepping into the classroom each morning, I wound my own key, then went in and performed. Each evening after the lights went off in the sophomore dorm, I collapsed and let the voices subsume me. Anna's voice especially fed my passivity.

I became desperate—a heap of shards. I feared that I was so far along the road to craziness that I'd soon collapse into babbling. I never cried and yet inside I was sobbing a deep pool of despair. My mind was slipping away. The effort to teach took all the energy I had. When, I wondered, would the hallucinations become so vivid I'd begin to respond out loud to those three presences? When that happened, Mother Mary Sybil would send me to a mental ward. I'd spend the rest of my life sitting by a window, facing the sun's warmth, totally incoherent.

Niggling at my mind was the realization that I no longer thought of the presences as hallucinations. They were as real to me as the students. We engaged in conversations. I entered their arguments. I endured Anna's carping, welcomed Dolores's dulcet voice, and indulged Dodo's belief that everything in the firmament was "fine and dandy like sugar candy."

From my knowledge of its history, only a handful of professed nuns had left St. Cordelia Convent in the preceding 103 years. I'd heard a rumor that Sister Mary Paulus—who'd been professed longer than I—had left a few weeks before. That gave me hope that I, too, could leave. That seemed my only recourse.

Shortly before midnight on Monday, December 5, 1966, I walked, accompanied by the presences, to the choir chapel. There we knelt, my mind mired in a quicksand of questions: What of my vows? I meant them when I'd taken them. What of serving others? What of being a saint?

Always I came back to the person I had come to detest. My fractured soul was splintering. I had to leave or endure a breakdown. All the nuns, all the students, everyone would know just what a failure I was as a human being. I'd be incarcerated in a mental hospital the rest of my life.

On that December night, the three presences and I rose from the kneeler and left behind the chapel where I'd prayed for eight and a half years. Entering the shadowed convent hall, I shuffled to Mother Mary Sybil's office. Her face reflected surprise when I knocked on her open door.

She invited me in; I crossed the room and knelt at her side. I felt phlegmatic. Well, perhaps that's not correct. I felt ready for the floor to split open and tumble me into oblivion. "Mother Mary Sybil," I said, "I have to leave. I can't do this anymore. I need to leave."

She gazed down into my face for what seemed an eternity. Then she said, "Let's keep you in the academy until Christmas. Then in January I'll send you out to another mission to teach. Can you do that?"

"No." My head started to shake in denial. Then my whole body began to shake. I couldn't stop its trembling as tears coursed down my cheeks. "I have to leave the convent," I whimpered.

"Please, Sister Innocence, can you explain yourself?"

With words tumbling over one another I catalogued my ineptitudes: I was an ineffectual teacher. Inferior. I couldn't live the vow of obedience. I trusted my own will before others. I thought unkind thoughts all the time. Judgmental thoughts. I tried not to—the words were coming faster now, slipping over one another—I knew I was at fault. I simply acted a role. Other nuns thought I was someone I wasn't. My words slowed to a trickle as I slumped forward. My forehead came to rest against the edge of her desk as I whispered, "I just can't live this life anymore."

She began to pat my shoulder, saying, "It's all right. Everything is all right."

When I heard those words, I tried to kneel upright again. "No," I said, "nothing is right for me right now. Nothing."

She listened intently, her right hand on my shoulder. Then she reached into her pocket and drew out her handkerchief. Handing it to me, she said, "Would you be willing to take a leave of absence for a year? That way you could see if a life beyond the convent suited you."

Just the idea of getting away, of breathing free air again, of not feeling bound in, encompassed by the convent walls, lifted my spirits. "Yes," I said. "Okay."

"Before that happens," she continued, "I'd like you to speak with a counselor."

"Someone in town?"

"No. A monk who counsels other nuns here at the convent. You could tell him what you've shared with me."

"I'll still get to leave?" I felt panic.

"Yes. If that's your final decision you will. The question is—Do you want to take a leave of absence to consider your decision?"

I took a deep breath and swiped the handkerchief across my face. Then I looked up into her kind eyes and whispered, "Thank you. I will take that leave of absence."

Suddenly I realized I'd forgotten the students. "I'd like to finish off the topics the seniors are studying in English Lit and also to make out their grades for this semester," I said, hoping suddenly that, having made my decision, the convent wouldn't thrust me out in the next few days.

Mother Mary Sybil's smile was tired as she said, "I'd appreciate that."

"I'll hand in the grades on December 23. May I leave the next day?"

"You may."

Before I left her office, she gave me her blessing and asked that I write a letter formally requesting a leave of absence.

Returning to my room, I felt broken, not so much by the convent but by my own futile struggle to create nirvana in the midst of the gathering of humanity in which I found myself. The nuns and the convent had welcomed me more than eight years before. I had known mostly kindness from everyone I met and any unkindness was of no importance now. Prayer had sustained me, but I was so far short of perfection.

As I settled again into bed, memories inundated me—times of joy in the convent as well as sorrow. It had been both my life and my home for eight and a half years. How could I leave? Yet how could I not? I sobbed, pressing my face into the pillow so I wouldn't wake any of the sophomores who slept beyond the wall.

Then I remembered what Mom had told me the summer before—that I'd laid hold of the plow and had to forge ahead. Would she and Dad welcome me home? Or would they disown me? And if they did, where would I go? I had no money for rent or food or clothes. How would I even get from the convent to the town where I grew up with no money to buy a train ticket? Fear overwhelmed me. Maybe I couldn't leave the convent because I didn't have a job to earn any money. What was I going to do?

Alarmed, I left my room and rushed to the payphone in the alcove next to the fourth-floor elevator. Reversing the charges, I called home. Despite the lateness of the night, Mom answered and immediately accepted the charges when the operator spoke to her. "Dolores," she said. "What's happened?"

I sobbed uncontrollably.

"What is it? Tell me what's wrong?" she begged

I took a deep breath, trying to still the sobs and speak. "Mom," I mumbled. "Mom. I'm leaving the convent. I can't do this anymore. I just can't, Mom. Will you let me come home?"

"Honey, of course. We'll come up and get you tomorrow. What time? Is nine too early?"

"Not tomorrow, Mom. Wait 'til Christmas Eve morning. I need to finish off the course work for the students. And do the grades."

"What time?"

"After breakfast. Maybe around ten."

At the finality of those plans I sobbed in earnest. I could hear Mom saying, over and over, like a mantra, the words that Mother Mary Sybil had said only minutes before, "It's all right, Honey. It's all right." When my sobbing ebbed, she asked, gently, "Why don't we come and get you tomorrow?"

"I have to finish my teaching." I took great gulps of air. "I need to go to bed, Mom. You will come? You will, won't you?"

"Yes. Ten o'clock on December 24. We'll be there. We'll get you home where you'll be safe."

Before she hung up, I remembered that I would need clothes to wear home. "I'll ask your sister-in-law," she said. "She's pregnant and her clothes don't fit any more. I'm sure she'll lend them to you."

We said goodbye and I returned to my room, content that I could at least see as far as the morning of December 24.

Stalemate

The next afternoon I met with the monk who was to be my counselor and told him why I wanted to leave the convent. After I finished my dismal recitation, he said, "You need more fortitude than you've shown. You seem unwilling to persevere through the hard times."

His words confirmed my belief that I was a poor excuse for a nun. Recognizing the façade I wore, he said nothing more for a few moments and then asked, "You have rarely mentioned the community. Do you want to be a part of this community? Do you want to contribute to it?"

The two questions stalled my thinking. When I'd sorted through all the concerns I'd pondered for years, I had to admit that I had little concern about community. I was much more concerned about my becoming a saint.

As I explained this, he began to shake his head, seeming to reject my words. Then he said, "Perhaps you truly don't have a vocation. If you did you'd be less concerned about yourself and more concerned about the community."

Feeling dismal, I nodded, my eyes starting to water.

"The truth may be, Sister Innocence, that you are perhaps too self-centered for the convent. Too self-absorbed."

Acknowledging the truth of that, I thanked him for his counsel, asked for his blessing, and left the room. I suppose that he reported our session to Mother Mary Sybil. I don't know. I know only that she summoned me to her office on December 8, the Feast of the Immaculate Conception, and asked, "Do you still want to leave, Sister Innocence?"

"I do."

"In June you told Mother Mary Maude to ignore any decision you made to leave. You've definitely changed your mind?"

"I just can't do this anymore."

I saw some sudden emotion change her expression. *Anger* I thought, then asked myself why wouldn't she be angry? I was casting aside the vows I'd made. We looked at one another, both of us caught up now in this quagmire of what had been an ongoing struggle for me from as early as the novitiate days.

Mother Mary Sybil wasn't angry, however. When she spoke again, she simply repeated her suggestion that I take a year's leave of absence and then reassess my decision. I agreed. I just wanted to get away. Somehow. In some way. I wanted to run as fast as I could from the hold monasticism had on me.

During the rest of that week and for the following days until departure, I taught with renewed vigor. I participated devoutly in the monastic prayer of Benedictines. I listened intently to the students asking for advice.

I did all that was asked of me, yet I had no feelings; ice blocked them. I simply acted a role. It was a performance. I had no appetite and wasn't sleeping. From Thanksgiving on, I walked as the living dead—a zombie. But . . . always a zombie accompanied by three haunting presences.

A day or two before I left the convent, Sister Mary Nathan, my first mission superior, summoned me to her subprioress office. As I knelt by her desk, she expressed concern over my leaving. I just looked at her, unmoved by the memories of our life together on my first mission and her kindness and wisdom at that time. When this woman, whom I so respected, tried to probe my reasons for leaving, I said only, "I have to." As she came up with reason after reason for staying, I simply reiterated those words.

Finally, she said, "Sister Innocence, think of your mother and father. They made vows and kept them all these years. You must do the same."

"Sister Mary Nathan, many more times than once I begged my mother to leave my father."

"You may have begged, but she stayed true to her vows. She stayed with your father. Even in the hard times. That's what you need to do now. Whatever is bothering you will pass."

I knelt there, shaking my head, then muttered, "Her staying wasn't the right thing to do. His drinking affected all of us. I still think she should have left him and taken my brother and me with her."

For several more minutes she tried to make her point in other ways. Nothing she said impinged because I was hanging on by a thread. I had to leave. In the fog that filled my brain I could see only an open door that promised air I could breathe.

On December 23, a Friday, Mother Mary Sybil summoned me to her office. There I read and signed the following document, which gave me permission to leave the convent for a year.

> Sister M. Innocence (Dolores) Ready, O.S.B., of [St. Cordelia Convent] by letter of December 5, 1966, has, for a just cause, requested permission to live outside the religious community for a year.
>
> By reason of the authority granted to Major Superiors by the Holy See through #4 of the Decree to Lay Religious Institutes, I am, with the consent of my Council, granting you permission to be absent from the Religious House for not more than a year.
>
> You will be expected to put off the religious habit when you leave, and when you have established yourself in some location will notify the Ordinary of the place of your state as an excloistered religious and will be subject to him in obedience.
>
> Although an adequate sum is given by the Community to cover your immediate needs, you will be expected to seek suitable employment and thus to maintain yourself throughout the year.
>
> May God be pleased to show you His will and to grant you peace.
>
> Approved by the Council [of St. Cordelia Convent] this 20th day of December, 1966.

Mother signed the document, then I signed and dated the following sentence: "On this date, December 23, 1966, I accept the permission for exclaustration for one year as indicated above."

One of the vows I'd taken in final profession on January 1, 1963, was that of "stability." That is, I would be a part of that community of Benedictines for the rest of my life. As I walked away for a year, I needed permission to depart the convent and leave the Community.

The document I signed stated that the Community would give me "an adequate sum" for my immediate needs. But because of some mix-up, the bursar didn't give me any money before I left; I'd be totally dependent on my parents until I got a job. That loomed ahead, but no concerned thoughts formed in my dulled brain about it. My numbness obliterated past, present, future.

On that same day, Mother Mary Sybil wrote me a personal letter.

> Dear Sister Innocence,
>
> Late as it is, I cannot resist writing a brief note to you. In my own name and that of the Community, I wish to express my appreciation for the contribution you have made to our apostolic work.
>
> Even though you are leaving us, please be assured that the . . . Benedictines are not breaking their bond with you. You will be included daily in our remembrance of the "absent brethren."
>
> Know too, Sister, that I have faith in you as a person. I believe that you are trying sincerely to bear witness to Christ in the way that seems best for you. Know also, Sister, that if after you have tried to live outside the convent and find that you would like to return, we will gladly welcome you back. In the interim we will always have a prayerful and loving remembrance of you.
>
> I hope you will find the peace and happiness that you are seeking. God bless you through the coming year. Please remember me and the Community in your prayers.
>
> With love in the Holy Child, . . .

Before turning off the lights that evening, I read the letter with only a cursory nod of recognition for both the words and their sentiment. I simply held in my hand a piece of paper with scratching on it. Nothing there touched the icy core of my being or invaded my passivity. I'd lost my ability both to feel and to keep track of the passage of time. I felt warped. Placing the letter in my daily prayer book, I forgot about it.

I taught until the students left for Christmas vacation, then graded their finals. On the morning of Saturday, December 24, I placed a list of their grades on the desk of the academy principal. Then I participated in the Divine Office and Mass in the choir chapel. Like a puppet, whose strings were mechanically pulled, I chanted, prayed, knelt, bowed, praised, lifted my voice in song. All automatic. Prayer meant nothing, nor did the God who no longer held me dear.

Afterward, I processed with the rest of the nuns to the dining room. In silence, we ate our breakfast. Apathy glazed both my mind and my actions. When I'd finished the meal, I rerolled my silverware in the napkin, bound it with the initialed strip, and placed it with those of the nuns who were not at home that day.

I didn't need to do that; I could have simply taken the silverware with me. I wasn't trying to show the other nuns how brave I was. I was just one of the living dead trying to do the right thing clear up to the end.

At the time, I didn't know if anyone there was aware I was leaving, but as I walked down the hall toward Mother Mary Sybil's office, I saw that passing nuns looked at me strangely. Was that true? I don't know. I know only that my three presences accompanied me to that meal and down that hallway. Anna criticized me for being melodramatic. Dolores said, "Give her some slack." Dodo, playing hopscotch as we walked down the hall, sang out, "It's going to be a great adventure."

I knocked and entered Mother Mary Sybil's office. Kneeling for the last time, I asked her blessing on what I was doing.

She gave it and said, "I hope you come to some peace, Dee. I hope that we will see you back here in a year. But whatever happens, I wish you well."

She said a few more words, blessing my journey and praying that in the coming year I'd find the answers I sought. I left her office aware that I was the one leaving the convent; it wasn't abandoning me.

Certain that despite having a year to make up my mind, I would never return and resume my life as a nun, I walked the long hall from the motherhouse into the college administration building. I wanted to say goodbye to Sister Ellie, my college mentor.

For once when I knocked on her office door and entered the room, she was the only one sitting there. She rose and came forward. Taking my hand, she gazed at me as if trying to dive into the essence of my leaving. We stood there for long moments, both of us silent. Then she asked, "Whatever happened to the bright and shiny star you were?"

The convent happened.

But I didn't say that. I faulted myself more than she did. Others stayed—over six hundred of them. What was wrong with me? Why did I have no stick-to-it-ive-ness?

I said nothing to this woman whose nurturing in college had steadied me. I merely went out the door and left the convent behind. I didn't even knock on Sister Claude's office door as I passed it. I was so encased in ice that thanking her for all she'd done for me in the past four months—her thoughtful listening and her taking care of me during Thanksgiving vacation—never occurred to me.

Outside the college administration building, my parents awaited me in their sun-faded Chevrolet. Mom got out with the suitcase she'd brought. In it, she'd packed the clothes my pregnant sister-in-law was loaning me. She offered to walk with me to a room in a nearly college residence hall where I'd change into a lay person's clothing. I refused her offer because I was so used to privacy when I robed and disrobed. I saw the look of sorrow on her face as she leaned down to kiss my cheek.

"We'll be waiting for you here," she said. "There's no hurry. Take your time."

I walked away from her and entered the residence and then the room to which Mother Mary Sybil had directed me. I laid the suitcase on the bed. Then I turned toward the mirror atop the three-drawer dresser in the room. For the final time, I unpinned my headwear—the black outer veil, the shorter inner veil, the starched band that had always cut into my forehead, the coif, and the skullcap. Reverently, I laid each item on the bed. I turned hesitantly toward the dresser. Its mirror reflected a haggard face, the cheekbones prominent because of the weight I'd lost. My hair stuck up in tufts.

Next, I unhooked the shoulder of the long, black scapular. I stepped out of the habit I'd worn for eight years. With robotic precision, I put aside each piece of clothing. Those garments announced to the world that I was a nun. A Benedictine. They had defined me.

I stood like stone in my combination. Silent, I gazed dispassionately at the bony image reflected in the mirror. I didn't know who I was or what lay ahead. For so many weeks and months, I'd shuttered possibilities. I was a shell surrounding emptiness. A void. I was blank—no past, no future, just a timeless moment of inconsequence. Finally, I unsnapped the combination garment and stepped out of it.

I opened the suitcase then and touched the top item—a blouse. I had to think about each step of reclothing myself. What article of clothing went first? What second? Piece by piece, with great deliberation, I donned them. The feel of them was so different: The satin of underclothes. The crêpe of the blouse. The nubby wool of the skirt.

As I put on each piece of clothing, I felt myself taking one step after another in leaving the convent. The only thought I had was *There must be a right way to do this. To leave. Am I doing it the right way?*

After I had the clothes on, the mirror reflected a stranger. I knew what nuns looked like. This wasn't a nun. Then who was it? Whoever it was, she was scrawny. The street clothes sagged on her.

Again the thought came, *What's the right way to leave the convent? Anyone else would know. I don't. I'm ignorant about how to live life. I'm a failure.* The words echoed in a cavernous chamber of worthlessness. In the final days of teaching, I'd become aware that the jumbled thoughts in my head were unrelated to the words that slipped out of my mouth. An inner muteness settled in.

I stood before the mirror holding the makeup my sister-in-law had sent. I patted my cheeks with the power puff and blinked. I picked up the lipstick and wound the tube so that the red column appeared. I leaned toward the mirror. Hesitantly, I brought the tube closer and closer to my lips. I couldn't remember exactly how to put on lipstick. Should I purse my lips? Did I put it on while smiling? How had I done it when I was in college? I couldn't remember.

Mechanically I dabbed at my lips. Wearing lipstick was what women who weren't nuns did. I was leaving the convent, so this was what I was supposed to do. Finally, I stepped back and looked at myself in the mirror. I saw there a clown, lips painted garishly.

Turning, I placed my leave-of-absence document, my missal, my diurnal, and the letter from Mother Mary Sybil in the empty suitcase. As I picked it up, the articles inside shifted, banging its sides—so little to take home after so many years. I glanced around the room, entered the hallway, and lumbered out the door and down the sidewalk toward where Mom and Dad waited in the car.

Mom put the suitcase in the trunk of the car, then she and Dad tucked me between them in the front seat. Dad drove down the hill and headed home. For all of the two-hundred-and-fifty miles to the ramshackle house where I'd grown up, Mom held me close. Tenderly she brushed back my cowlick and wiped the tears that dribbled down my cheeks. As Dad patted my left knee with his right hand, driving with his left, he kept murmuring, "It's okay, honey. It's okay. We'll take care of you."

Mom muttered, "I knew that place would do you in."

My parents didn't know we weren't alone. In the back seat sat three presences, yammering at me: Anna. Dodo. Dolores. For the entire trip home, all three kept telling me just what they thought of my decision to leave and where it might lead me. Anna attacked. Dolores consoled. Dodo prattled on about the fun we'd have.

No respite from myself accompanied me home. My love of prayer hadn't been enough to strengthen my resolve to remain a nun. I was left with only the three presences—voices, faces, bodies. They, not prayer, were ever present.

Epilogue

And All Shall Be Well

Those three presences made my re-entry into secular life much more difficult than it would have had to be. Each time I engaged in a discussion with others, the presences commented on what I said, how I looked, and my facial expression. They judged my intelligence, my inanities, my sense of humor, the sound of my laughter, my uncertainties.

They yammered. Yammered. Yammered as I was trying to listen to the person or group with whom I was talking, even to the actors on the television screen. I had to work so hard to separate what the three were saying—in three different corners of whatever room I was in—from what was being said by the real-life person in front of me. Who said what? To which statement did I need to respond?

I wondered then if sometimes I spoke out loud to the three presences. What did the "real" people think if I did that? And what was real? Those presences were certainly real to me, but I was almost, but not quite, certain that they weren't real to anyone else. Unsure of who knew what, I kept quiet about them.

Within the first year of my leaving, I began seeing a psychiatrist, Dr. Gibson. Even though I trusted him and felt safe sharing my life with him, I didn't mention Anna, Dolores, and Dodo in our sessions because I lived with two fears, the second contingent on the first: If I told him, he'd have me committed to a mental hospital where I'd be held captive and possibly subjected to strange medications and machines, which terrified me.

The second fear was equally terrifying: What would remain of me if I lost Anna, Dolores, and Dodo? I knew the answer to that—

I'd be nothing; I'd disappear into nothingness. I was nothing without them.

So for years, Anna, Dolores, and Dodo remained my secret. A secret that exhausted me. All three blathered at me incessantly. Anna remonstrating. Scolding. Dolores suggesting compromise, trying to find some middle ground on which we could all agree. Dodo giggling at the daily events of my life.

I needed every particle of the energy within my body to be attentive to them as well as to the reality beyond them. Listening— without responding to those three presences, listening while needing to respond to the voices of tangible humans who now filled my life—exhausted me. I slept longer hours because tiredness had seeped into the marrow of my bones. Even breathing became arduous.

For nine years—from January 1967 to February 1976—those three and I explored life beyond the convent. We dated; shopped for colorful clothes; moved several times; had sessions with three psychiatrists in three different states; and made a multitude of friends with whom we enjoyed restaurants, concerts, and movies.

Together, we flew home to visit my parents; grieved when my mother died; consoled my father and brother. The four of us worked as an editor and curriculum developer; taught at two schools; and got a master's degree in American Studies. They accompanied me everywhere; they infiltrated every moment of my waking life. The only place they remained apart was in my dreams.

Despite their constant presence, life seemed full and rich for those nine years. Gone were the days when I was a mummy with an exterior wall of batting separating me from the world. I'd re-entered life and was—except for the hallucinations—mostly happy. Admittedly, I missed the many friends I'd made in the convent— women who laughed frequently, showed compassion toward all, and cared with deep concern about our world.

Still, I did not truly live as an integrated person until 1976 when I finally told the third psychiatrist about the three presences in my life. The medication she prescribed for psychosis led to their demise. Within a month I lived with only myself. From that time to this, I have seen them only when I went off the medication for a few days.

As the years passed, my career as a curriculum developer flourished. During the years between then and now, I've had periods of good health; periods of bad. I've made friends and enjoyed my life, while actively engaging in political protest and doing what I could during the AIDS epidemic here in the United States. But that span of years is another story for another time.

In June 2009, forty-three years after leaving the convent, I left the northern state where I'd lived and worked for most of those years. Because of ill health, I moved back to my hometown where my extended family lived. Settling here wasn't easy. Retired and not a joiner, I felt my life narrowing. Loneliness sapped the gift of each day.

The one activity that allayed my isolation was the craft of writing. I'd begun writing twenty years before when Dulcy, the cat with whom I'd lived for nearly two decades, channeled through me the story of our relationship.

In 1992, Crown had published her book, *A Cat's Life: Dulcy's Story*. Subsequently, many readers sent me letters in which they shared their own stories of living with cats. Reading those letters became part of the magic of being published.

Following the publication of Dulcy's book, I wrote daily, completing several manuscripts. None were published. Nevertheless, my persistent heartwish only deepened: I wanted to write the stories given me by the Universe and get those stories published. If I could do that, then a multitude of readers would meet the characters who peopled these manuscripts and come to care for them as I did.

Fortunately, a long-time friend offered a suggestion: "Dee, if you want to get published, write a memoir."

"Why? . . . My life's so ordinary."

"My life's ordinary," she countered. "Yours is interesting." Stunning moment.

As I somewhat hesitantly began to work on the memoir, I felt myself faltering frequently. Why? Why? Why had I left? After all these years I still didn't know. How could I write a memoir and bring no understanding to it? Then a freeing thought came: *Perhaps, just perhaps, the writing will bring understanding.*

As the writing days passed, I came to grips with the fear that had haunted me since leaving the convent—that Sister Innocence had been nothing but a fake all those years ago. She had no authenticity. Always as my mind roamed the past, I came back to that because leaving had always felt like an abysmal acceptance of failure.

Slowly, truthfully, very slowly, came the realization that although it's been nearly sixty years since I entered the convent—fifty-one since I left—I had a reason to write: I wanted to reclaim Sister Innocence. To befriend her. I felt that I had abandoned her and her heartwishes for decades of my life. It was time to embrace her and all her foibles, her faults, her deep woundedness.

As I've written these past months, the truth of my eight-and-a-half years in the convent has slowly emerged. What has also happened is that I can finally articulate why being in the convent didn't work for me. These realizations have come because I've finally been able to understand what monasticism is.

As early as the third century CE, many Christians felt drawn to a life of prayer and asceticism. Some went out into the deserts of Palestine and Egypt, away from the hubbub of settlement. These hermits, be they men or women, sought the presence of God in solitude. Within such a life, however, lurks the crippling possibility of becoming self-absorbed, self-centered, selfish. One can lose his or her willingness to engage in the give-and-take of human relationships.

Human beings are social creatures. Rubbing up against one another's messiness helps all of us become whole. The interplay of resolving communal differences promotes emotional growth. The community doing this may be a committed couple, a family with children, an extended family, friendships, a monthly book club, a town, a city, a nation.

Out of the many, one group forms.

Those within each group must contend with one another's shortcomings. Letting go of our own will and compromising with these flaws is difficult—at least it was for me. Benedict was not speaking only of physical labor when he stressed the motto "Ora et Labora," that is, "pray and work." Building community takes work. It takes a willingness to pray for those who annoy us. It asks us to compromise our own dream of what the convent needs to be.

I entered the convent unaware of this. I didn't enter because I wanted to be part of community—which is what monasticism is all about. Instead, I entered solely to praise God, but I didn't realize that praise takes many forms. It is not only *ora*—prayer. It is also embracing the tension of community—*labora*—and offering that to God.

I also wanted Oneness, but I didn't understand the implications of that word. I didn't realize that living in Oneness meant embracing differences. I was naïve. Immature. Idealistic.

When praying the Divine Office, I found the serenity I sought. In the daily life of the convent, however, I met the reality of over six hundred women living together. The composition of a convent is like any small or large group of people whether it be a platoon, a law office, a free clinic for the inner city poor, a union of construction workers, a fraternal order of like-minded philanthropists, a state legislature, a troop of scouts, a band of mountain climbers.

How does the group become One? Community grows out of shared vision and the willingness to compromise and let go of self-absorption. What is asked of each community member is the willingness to place the good of the whole before the doggedness of any one member of the group.

Yet each member of that group is an individual with mood swings, needs, and dreams that differ from those of others. Some members are mean-spirited; some, abrasive; some see only good; some see only fault; some judge others and find them wanting; some—like myself—seek an unrealistic peace. From the beginning I misunderstood the intent of monasticism. I was reluctant to embrace the demands of communal living. I wanted to be free from choosing the will of others over my own. The outcome of my recalcitrance? I left the convent.

For several years after leaving, I lost the hope that I would ever grow up and come to grips with why I left. I lost also the hope that I'd ultimately become a saint. I wasn't perfect, and if being perfect was the only way to win the love of others, then I'd have to relinquish that too.

For many, many years I lived a life of emotional immaturity. That provides much of the reason for why the decision to share this story came fifty years after leaving the convent. That much time had to pass before I could forgive myself and embrace this person who sits before this computer and writes on a hot, windless day in September 2017.

This memoir has helped me understand my own strength, fortitude, and determination—my will to survive. In one of his poems, Robert Browning wrote, "On the earth the broken arcs; in the heaven, a perfect round." What I have discovered in my writing is that the convent was an arc of my life, not the perfect round.

I would never want to cast a negative light on the convent or the nuns with whom I lived. All who entered came to dedicate their lives to service and to praise the deep dark God who called them. They answered that call with great fortitude and goodwill. They ran forward to embrace their vocations.

Yet we were all simply human. My failing then and often throughout my life is that I've demanded from others and from myself that we be more than simply human. We had to be perfect in every way. Again and again I've been unable to accept the frailties within myself and others.

Walt Whitman wrote, "The words of my book nothing, the drift of it everything." In this memoir I've grappled with the drift of my life in the convent and found its meaning: the convent is the place where I began to grow up and where I received a foundation in my lifelong search for social justice and peace. I now want to share those long-ago days of darkness and of light in a Benedictine convent.

I hope that this memoir has spoken to you of a young, immature woman who longed to pray and who found herself spiraling into psychosis because she could not accept others as they were, nor could she accept herself. Always she wanted a perfection from them that eluded her own self.

I hope also that this memoir will bless all of you who have traveled back with me to a time of innocence when I tried to embrace a world of my own imagination and leave reality behind.

Peace.

Acknowledgments

Two friends—Yvette Nelson and Jerri Farris—prompted my memoir writing. I thought both of them were talking nonsense when they encouraged me to write about my life. Having now completed the convent part, I find myself deeply grateful to them. They have helped me reclaim Sister Innocence, whom I deserted on Christmas Eve 1966.

I want to thank them and all the other friends who, for a multitude of years, have steadfastly believed in my dream of being published. One of them—LeaAnn Gregerson— tells me each time we talk that I'm a wonderful writer. Her words always make my sagging spirits soar.

I feel deeply grateful to all the people who physically helped get my book ready for publication either by reading the manuscript in its various drafts or by producing the final product: Fran Fischer, Lisa Crumley, Debra Fetterly, Judy Healey, Judy King, Sally Brewer Lawrence, Dr. Kathy McCoy, Jeanne Peltier, Linda Smitka, and Ruby Stilson.

Finally, I want to express thanksgiving for my parents who repeatedly said two things to me as I grew up: "Dolores, you can do anything you set your mind to," and "You find what you look for. If you look for good, you will find it, and if you look for bad, you will surely find that too." Those words filled me with hope when I was a child; they continue to do so. The blessing of having Mom and Dad as my parents is immeasurable and never-ending.

Peace.

Find Dee Ready Online

Website: www.DeeReady.com

Facebook: www.facebook.com/DeeReadyaspiringnovelist

Blog: cominghometomyself.blogspot.com

Twitter: @dee_ready36

75551517R00124

Made in the USA
San Bernardino, CA
01 May 2018